Developing Reading COMPREHENSION SKILLS

SKILLS

FOR KEY STAGE 3 TESTS

CLARE CONSTANT · DAVID KITCHEN · MARK MORRIS

Heinemann Educational Publishers
Halley Court, Jordan Hill, Oxford OX2 8EJ
A division of Reed Educational and Professional
Publishing Ltd

OXFORD MELBOURNE AUCKLAND JOHANNESBURG
BLANTYRE GABORONE
IBADAN PORTSMOUTH (NH) USA CHICAGO

First published 2000

04 03 02 01 00

10 9 8 7 6 5 4 3 2 1

ISBN 0 435 10831X

Acknowledgements

The authors and Publishers wish to thank the following
for kindly granting permission to include copyright
material:

Rogers, Coleridge & White Ltd. on behalf of Kevin
Crossley-Holland for an extract from *Boo!* published by
Orchard Books; Egmont Children's Books Ltd. for an
extract from *The Mysterious Mr Ross* by Vivien Alcock ©
1987, published by Methuen Children's Books and
Mammoth, imprints of Egmont Children's Books Ltd;
CitizenCard for their leaflet; BBC for their Online Web
Guide 'Celebrity Choice' ref: www.bbc.co.uk/webguide,
and SFX Sports Group on behalf of Gary Lineker; News
International Newspapers Ltd. for the headline 'I'm fur-
reezing' by Caroline Sigley in *The Sun*, 13 June, 1999, ©;
News International Newspapers Ltd. for the headline
'Hamster that nearly had its chips' by Tracy Conner and
Nigel Hawkes in *The Times*, 23 June, 1999, ©; Skyline,
Professional Events Organisation, for their leaflet
'Wanted'; The Kingston Informer Newspaper for the
article 'I'm re-hearse-ing' by Daniel Abrahams, 28 May,
1998, ©; KJC Mobile Phones for their advertisement; Tesco
Stores Ltd. for the Tesconet advertisement in their
Clubcard Magazine; Ocean Marketing for the Advanced
Hair Studio advertisement; First Point International for
their advertisement 'A New Life Abroad!'; The Laser Clinic
for their advertisement 'Tattoo Removal'; Lever Brothers
Ltd. for their advertisement 'Persil makes your money go
round'; Reckitt Benckiser Plc for their 'Bracemate'
advertisement; Red Driving School Ltd. for their
advertisement; The Christopher Little Literary Agency on
behalf of J.K. Rowling for an extract from *Harry Potter
and the Philosopher's Stone* copyright © J.K. Rowling,
1997; Walker Books Ltd. for an extract from *The Changing
Face of Johnny Casanova* by Jamie Rix © 1998; Transworld
Publishing for an extract from *Johnny and the Bomb* by
Terry Pratchett, unadapted as requested; Egmont
Children's Books Ltd. for an extract from 'Touching
Greatness' from *One Step Beyond* by Pete Johnson, ©
1990, published by Mammoth, an imprint of Egmont
Children's Books Ltd; Oxford University Press for an
extract from *Firebug* by Susan Gates; Vernon Scannell for
his poem 'Jason's Trial'; Paul Cookson 'Coolscorin'
Matchwinnin' Celebratin' Striker'; David R. Morgan for his
poem 'The Hedgehog Warns Her Children'; Macmillan
Children's Books for an extract from *The Swap* by George
Layton; Penguin Books Australia Ltd. for an extract from
Uncanny by Paul Jennings; Bloomsbury Publishing Plc for
an extract from *Zeebrugge; A Hero's Story* by Stephen
Homewood, 1998; Laura Cecil Literary Agency on behalf
of the Estate of Robert Westall for an extract from 'The
Ruined City of Kor' in *Blitz*, © 1995; News International
Newspapers Ltd. for the article 'Goldfish rescued from
tree' by Alastair Taylor in *The Sun*, 4 August, 1998, ©; The
Peters Fraser and Dunlop Group on behalf of Roger
McGough for his poem 'US Flies in Hamburgers' in *A
World of Poetry* published by Kingfisher; Sight Savers
International for their advertisement 'It's what all the girls
are wearing these days'; International Thomson
Publishing Services for an extract from the play *No Man's
Land* by Paul Swift, published by Thomas Nelson, 1993;
Hamish Hamilton Ltd. for an extract from *Step by Wicked
Step* by Anne Fine, © 1995; John Foster for his poem 'Fox
Farm' © 1991, from *Four O'clock Friday* published by
Oxford University Press; Save the Children for their 1997
leaflet 'Save the Children UK'; Hodder & Stoughton
Educational for an extract from 'Fat Boy With a Trumpet'
in *Fearsome Tales for Fiendish Kids*; Methuen Publishing
Ltd. for an extract from the play *Junk* by Melvin Burgess,
adapted by John Retallack; Siguy Films Ltd. for extracts
from the transcripts of the BBC programme, 'Money,
Money, Money' June/July, 1999; Moira Andrew for her
poem 'Child with a Cause'; Faber and Faber Ltd. for an
extract from *Andi's War* by Billy Rosen; Transworld
Publishers for an extract from *The Lost Continent* by Bill
Bryson, © 1989, published by Black Swan, a division of
Transworld Publishers. All rights reserved; Anderson Press
Ltd. for an extract from *Junk* by Melvin Burgess; The
Children's Society for an extract from their leaflet '£5
could buy this street survival kit'; Piccadilly Press for an
extract from *Sussed and Streetwise* by Jane Goldman;
Transworld Publishers for an extract from *Thief!* by
Malorie Blackman.

Whilst every effort has been made to locate the
owners of copyright in some cases this has been
unsuccessful. The publishers apologise for any
omission of original sources and will be pleased to
make the necessary arrangements at the first
opportunity.

The Publishers would like to thank the following for
permission to reproduce photographs on the pages
noted:

BBC Photolibrary, p8; News International, p19;
Matthew Pover, p19; Andy Lynn, p23; Rex
Features/SIPA, pp66-67; Trevor Clifford, p74; J. Allan
Cash, p99; Siguy Films/ Trevor Clifford, pp114-115;
J. Allan Cash, p127.

Original design by 320 Design, Tatsfield, Kent

Designed and produced by Moondisks Ltd, Cambridge

Printed and bound in Spain by Edelvives

Original illustrations © Heinemann Educational
Publishers 2000

Illustrations by Mik Brown, Tim Kahane, Avril
Turner/Linda Rogers Associates, Peter Richardson, Peter
Rees/Linda Rogers Associates

Introduction

This book aims to help you develop your reading and understanding skills when approaching a wide variety of texts at Key Stage 3. It will enable you to build on skills you already have and develop some new ones.

Working through the units will give you confidence that you can respond well to any texts you are given during Key Stage 3, in tests or later in your GCSE classes.

You may have wondered:

- What am I supposed to be looking for when I read a poem or a text?
- How do I work out how an advertisement persuades people?
- What is the difference between a fact and an opinion?
- How do I make the best use of my time in an exam?

You will find the answers to these and many other questions in this book. Using it will make sure you can read and understand any type of reading matter and enjoy what you read.

Section A teaches the skills you need to read different kinds of texts.

Section B gives you practice in reading and understanding fiction, non-fiction, poetry, drama, information and media texts. The texts and questions become more demanding throughout this section.

Section C helps you to prepare to read texts and answer questions on them under timed conditions.

Contents

Section C: Tests

A1 Readers matter

Words are everywhere. Written words work together to make a text for someone to read. Find out what a text is doing by asking these three questions:

1   *What* is the text about?
      This tells you its ⓒontent.

2   *Who* was the text written for?
      This tells you its ⓐudience.

3   *How* would the writer like the
      reader to respond?   *This tells you its* ⓟurpose.

1   Read the texts on the opposite page.

2   What is each text about? (*What is its content?*) Write *one* sentence about each text. The first one has been done for you.

Text A is a news story about teenagers having to be home by nine o'clock.

Text B is …

3   Who was each text written for? (*Who is its audience?*) How do you know that it is meant for them? Copy out and complete the chart below.

Text type	Audience	It's meant for them because …
A Newspaper article	Teenagers	It says 'If you're a teenager …'
B		It says 'Pictures of Top Premiership Players'.

4   How would the writer of each text like the reader to respond? (*What is its purpose?*) Use the words below to help you explain the purpose of each text.

| find   buy   watch   invite |
| enjoy   work   worry   understand |

The purpose of the newspaper article A is to make teenagers … because it says …

A

HOME TIME FOR TEENAGERS

If you're a teenager reading this, check your watch. If it's after 9.00 pm you'd better be at home. The local council has brought in a tough new law. They have given the police power to arrest young people still out on the streets after nine o'clock. It's not just that your mum will have to pay a heavy fine. You might be made to work for local charities …

B

C

Outlook Express

Inbox

!	@	Subject	From	Date Sent
		Welcome to Outlook Express	Outlook Expr…	Wed, Nov 2…

```
Ryan
I'm not catching the train to Newton on Saturday. My
uncle is giving me a lift in earlier. Let's meet up
outside Spicer's Chippy at 1.00 pm before the match.
You'll need to turn left when you come out of the
train station. Then turn right at the traffic lights
and go all the way down the hill till you see Grove
Square. Spicer's is on the corner.
See you there
```

D

FILM VIEW *Frank's Fortune* ★★★★

It's laughter all the way for the whole family in the film *Frank's Fortune*. Nasty millionaire Jim Tarey is dying. His final trick is to tell his only son Frank what is in his will. His entire fortune will go to a hedgehog charity unless Frank enters the Winter Olympics and wins a medal.

Unfortunately Frank owes a lot of money to a ruthless criminal. The criminal will kill Frank if he doesn't pay him back. So Frank, even though he is hugely overweight and so short-sighted he talks to coat racks, does all he can to become a world-class skier.

Don't miss this film!

Mix and match

5   A new show called *Super Soap Star* is being shown on TV. Three magazine editors each want a piece written about it. Read what kind of text each editor is looking for. Then answer the questions that follow.

A

My readers enjoy television programmes that make them think! I want to warn them not to waste time watching the new show Super Soap Star!

B

My teenage readers love watching game shows. They always know what's going on in the soaps. I wouldn't want them to miss out on Super Soap Star.

C

My readers have a great sense of fun. They enjoy watching soaps and they'll do anything that's really wacky. They might want to be on Super Soap Star.

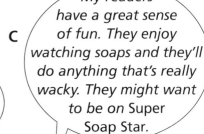

6   Read each text opposite. Which text would each editor print? Give a reason for your answer.

Editor A would choose text ... because ...

See page 6   7   Each editor is looking for a heading to go with their text. Which heading should each choose? Give a reason for your answer.

Editor A should choose heading ... because ...

8   Now look at the pictures below. Which picture should each editor choose to go with their article? Give a reason for your answer.

1

2

3

TEXTS

1 'You could be our Super Soap Star!'
Don't know what I'm talking about? Then grab the remote control at 8.00 pm on Friday night and flick over to Channel S.

Yes, I admit it. I watched their new soap game show and I'm hooked!

Finger on the buzzer quizzes find out if contestants know their Rovers Return from their Queen Vic. Then they get the chance to imitate a well known soap star. I laughed so much at last week's Peggy Mitchell look-alike contest I almost ...

Even my Dad was rolling on the floor when the final two contestants tried to take a starring role in *Neighbours*!

The prizes are pretty cool. The pace is frantic. It's just hysterical. Watch it!

10/10

2 **You could be our Super Soap Star!**
Channel S are showing an exciting new quiz show and they're looking for more people to take part.

The prizes are fantastic! The pace is furious! The fun is fabulous!
So if you ...
- ❖ know your Rovers Return from your Queen Vic
- ❖ can imitate a well known soap star
- ❖ long to take the starring role in a soap scene

call Ray on 0171 234 3543

3 'You could be our Super Soap Star!'

I do hope not! Channel S are showing a new quiz show and are scouring the country for soap freaks to go on it.

The first round is a dreary 'finger on the buzzer' quiz ... Do contestants know their Rovers Return from their Queen Vic? Do you care?

The next round is even worse. Can contestants do an appalling take-off of some sad soap star? Yes, unfortunately they can, but it's just so boring to watch.

The prizes are pathetic. The pace is sluggish. The fun fizzles out.

If ever there was a show to miss, it's *Super Soap Star*.

HEADINGS

1 Calling all Soap Experts! **2** Such Sad Soapies ...

3 Super Cool Soap!

A2 Reading prose

Sometimes you are given a piece of writing and asked to answer questions on it. Follow the four steps below to help you write good answers.

See page 6

Passage – read it through once to find out what it is about.

Questions – work out *what* you need to find out.

Re-read the whole passage again slowly and carefully. This time try to understand it as much as you can. Spot where the answers to the questions are.

Search in the *right* place for the *right* details to get the *right* answer to the first question. Repeat for the second question, and the third …

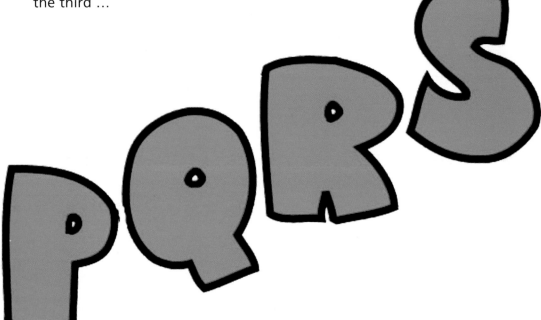

Reading fiction

Fiction is writing which has 'made up' events in it – such as a story. One of the main purposes of fiction is to entertain its readers.

1   Read the story below.

Boo!

She didn't like it at all when her father had to go down to London and, for the first time, she had to sleep alone in the old house.

She went up to her bedroom early. She turned the key and locked the door. She latched the windows and drew the curtains. She peered
5   inside her wardrobe, and pulled open the bottom drawer of her chest-of-drawers; she got down on her knees and looked under the bed.

She undressed; she put on her nightdress.

She pulled back the heavy linen cover and climbed into bed. Not to read but to try and sleep – she wanted to sleep as soon as she could.
10   She reached out and turned off the lamp.

'That's good,' said a little voice. 'Now we're safely locked in for the night.'

Boo! by Kevin Crossley Holland

When you answer these questions, don't forget to use PQRS!

2   Read lines 1–2. What is the girl worried about?

The girl is worried because she has to … and …

3   Read lines 3–10. List five ways the girl tries to make sure she is safe.

4   Read lines 11–12. Which statement below best explains the story's ending?

A   She goes to sleep without any problem.

B   Someone has broken into the house even though she locked the doors and latched the windows.

C   She did not realise someone was already in the house. When the person speaks you realise she has locked them both in the house, and she can't escape.

Most fiction is built up using three parts, in the same way as *Boo!*

Conflict	
In the beginning there is a problem which has to be overcome.	*The girl wants to sleep in the house on her own but she is afraid.*
Development of the problem	
In the middle part of the story the problem becomes more difficult.	*The girl has to work very hard to make sure she will be safe in the house.*
Resolution	
At the end of the story the problem comes to an end (one way or another). This is called the **resolution**.	*The stranger speaks and you realise she has locked them both in the house together. Now she cannot escape.*

1   Read the fiction passage opposite. Then copy out and complete the chart below to find out how it follows this pattern. Make sure you use PQRS.

Conflict	
• Read the introduction and lines 1–4. What problem does Felicity face?	Felicity wants to … but …
Development of the problem	
• Read lines 5–25. Which two events make things even harder for Felicity and Mr Ross?	
Resolution	
• Read lines 25–30. How has Felicity overcome the problem by the end of the story?	

🔑 Key points

When you answer a question:

- Do not just copy out large chunks of the text. Quote a **short** piece of text if you need to. (To find out more about quoting, see pages 56–57.)
- Explain the main part of the answer in your own words.

A stranger is sitting on a rock out at sea. The tide is coming in quickly. Felicity knows the stranger will drown unless he can reach the stick she is holding out.

Saving Mr Ross

'NOW!' she shouted.

He leaped down into the sea, his arm outstretched. The wood jerked wildly in her hand as he clung to it. He was coming towards her now. The stick twisted in her hands like a living thing. He was nearly there. He was smiling …

5   A wave slapped him, and he fell.

There was a last terrible pull on her arms. A sharp crack. Then nothing. The sea's roar died down. She had fallen back against the rock to which she still clung with one hand. In the other was a broken piece of wood. The man had gone.

10   He's drowned, she thought. He's drowned.

Then she saw fingers, pale as bone, clutching the edge of the dark stone by her feet. He began to pull himself up, his clothes soaked, his hair plastered to his head.

She caught hold of his arm and tugged, and then he was lying flat on the
15 rock, coughing and gasping for breath, as another wave rushed harmlessly past.

'Hurry! We're not safe yet. Come on, up there,' she pointed.

'I can't.'

'You've got to!' she shouted.

Then they had no breath for talking. Only when, at last, they were sitting on
20 top of the rockfall, shivering and clinging together, did they begin to chatter.

'My feet shot away. They simply shot away!' he said.

'I couldn't see you. I thought you'd drowned,' she said.

'It's the end, I thought, I'm done for.'

'Then I saw your hand –'

25 'Those rocks – is that blood on my face, or water?'

'Water, I think.'

'You saved my life,' the man said. There seemed to be tears in his eyes, or perhaps they were still wet from the sea.

'But the stick broke,' she said.

30 'You saved my life,' he insisted. 'I shall always remember.'

Adapted from *The Mysterious Mr Ross* *by Gillian Cross*

Reading non-fiction

Non-fiction is writing that deals with real events, people, places and facts. Its purpose is to inform or persuade.

You are going to look at a *leaflet* now. But you will meet different types of non-fiction in other units, such as *advertisements*, *articles*, *autobiography* and *travel writing*.

When you answer the questions below, remember to use your own words as much as possible.

See page 10

1   Read the non-fiction leaflet on the opposite page.

2   Read lines 1–4.

   a   How old do you need to be to buy your first CitizenCard?

   b   Who supports the CitizenCard scheme?

   c   How can showing a CitizenCard help some people to buy certain goods?

3   Read lines 7–17.

   a   What else does having a CitizenCard give you?

   b   How can you find out more about CitizenCard?

4   Work in pairs. What could you say to persuade each person below to buy a CitizenCard?

A   I get served in our local pub in Sussex because they know me. But the other day I tried to buy my girlfriend a drink in her local in Leeds. I got thrown out because I don't look 18! I don't want that happening again.

B   I'm so hard up. I'm not spending £5 if all a CitizenCard does is prove I'm 13.

The Old Soak

BUS STOP

CitizenCard™
The Retail Proof of Age Scheme

APPLICATION FORM

CitizenCard™ is the national proof of age scheme for anyone 12 years old or over in Britain and Ireland. You can buy six separate age cards at ages 12, 14, 15, 16, 18+ and 21+.

5 CitizenCard is a non-profit scheme supported by thousands of shops, pubs, supermarkets, betting shops and off-licences. Staff in these outlets will sell age-restricted products and services if a CitizenCard is shown. A first card costs £5 and a

10 renewal costs £3. Every card gives:

Proof of Age

Free Voicemail Service

Free Phone Calls

Discount Vouchers

You can make five minutes of free national phone calls with a card, after which you can buy more phonetime. Friends can leave messages on your voicemail, and the discount vouchers will save

15 you pounds off music, sport and other goods.

For information call 0870 240 1221 or visit www.citizencard.net.

A3 Reading media and information texts

Finding your way around

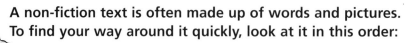

> A non-fiction text is often made up of words and pictures.
> To find your way around it quickly, look at it in this order:
>
> **H** Headings – main headings and subheadings. They tell you what each part of the text is about.
>
> **I** Illustrations – look at each picture and then read its description (*caption*).
>
> **P** Prose – there may be several chunks of writing to read. Use the method you learned on page 10.

Internet website

1 Read the text opposite. It is from a website on the Internet. Then answer the questions below using full sentences.

  a Look at the three subheadings. What do they tell you?

  The three subheadings tell you which websites Gary Lineker likes best.

  b What does the illustration show you?

  c What does the prose in **bold** tell you?

  d What does each of the other sections of prose tell you?

2 Now answer these questions. Write in full sentences.

  a What is Gary Lineker's new television series about?

  Gary Lineker's new television series is about …

  b Why does Gary like golf?

  c Which disease did Gary's son, George, suffer from?

  d What did Gary's sons believe about other children's fathers?

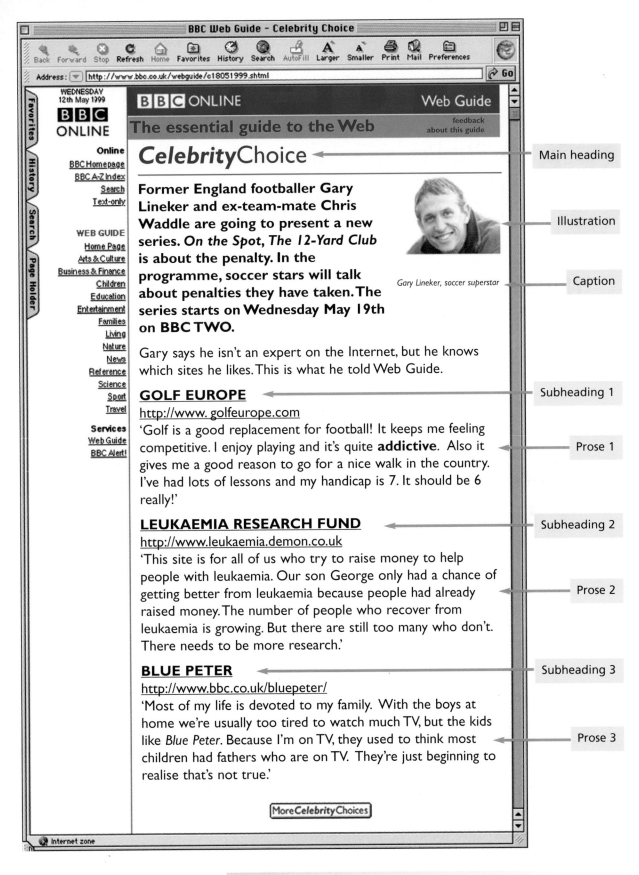

Main heading

Illustration

Caption — Gary Lineker, soccer superstar

BBC ONLINE — Web Guide

The essential guide to the Web
feedback
about this guide

*Celebrity*Choice

Former England footballer Gary Lineker and ex-team-mate Chris Waddle are going to present a new series. *On the Spot, The 12-Yard Club* is about the penalty. In the programme, soccer stars will talk about penalties they have taken. The series starts on **Wednesday May 19th** on **BBC TWO.**

Gary says he isn't an expert on the Internet, but he knows which sites he likes. This is what he told Web Guide.

GOLF EUROPE — Subheading 1
http://www. golfeurope.com
'Golf is a good replacement for football! It keeps me feeling competitive. I enjoy playing and it's quite **addictive**. Also it gives me a good reason to go for a nice walk in the country. I've had lots of lessons and my handicap is 7. It should be 6 really!' — Prose 1

LEUKAEMIA RESEARCH FUND — Subheading 2
http://www.leukaemia.demon.co.uk
'This site is for all of us who try to raise money to help people with leukaemia. Our son George only had a chance of getting better from leukaemia because people had already raised money. The number of people who recover from leukaemia is growing. But there are still too many who don't. There needs to be more research.' — Prose 2

BLUE PETER — Subheading 3
http://www.bbc.co.uk/bluepeter/
'Most of my life is devoted to my family. With the boys at home we're usually too tired to watch much TV, but the kids like *Blue Peter*. Because I'm on TV, they used to think most children had fathers who are on TV. They're just beginning to realise that's not true.' — Prose 3

More*Celebrity*Choices

Address: http://www.bbc.co.uk/webguide/c18051999.shtml

WEDNESDAY 12th May 1999

Online
BBC Homepage
BBC A-Z Index
Search
Text-only

WEB GUIDE
Home Page
Arts & Culture
Business & Finance
Children
Education
Entertainment
Families
Living
Nature
News
Reference
Science
Sport
Travel

Services
Web Guide
BBC Alert!

addictive: *makes you want to do it more and more*

Appearance

How a media or information text *looks* is important, as well as what it says.

Think about where these are on the page and what effect they have:

Headings – main headings and subheadings.

Illustrations – both the picture and the caption (its *description*).

Prose – there may be several chunks of writing.

Newspaper article

1   Read the text opposite. The same news story was printed in two different newspapers. Look at how each text was set out on the page.

2   Copy out and complete the chart below about each part of text **A**.

		Where is it on the page?	*What* does it make me notice?	*How* does it make me notice it?
H	Heading		how cold it is	it's large and …
I	Illustration		where the hamster …	you see the photo first …
P	Prose	in a chunk at the bottom with the picture above		it's like a stage the picture stands on.

3   Now copy out and complete a similar chart for each part of text **B**.

		Where is it on the page?	*What* does it make me notice?	*How* does it make me notice it?
H	Heading			
I	Illustration		the hamster	you see his …
P	Prose	at the side and …		it helps frame the …

4   Now look at both your charts. Which newspaper story was trying to do each of these jobs? Give reasons for your answer.

   a   Make you feel amazed that this hamster is still alive after three days in a freezer.

   b   Make you feel happy for the hamster that it was found alive.

A

I'M FUR-REEZING
Hamster lost for 3 days found in freezer

Heart-warming tale … missing Hamster Gizmo survived hidden away among the frozen food and is now fully recovered

Prawns

Lucky

Large, bold, eye-catching **headline**.

Photo shows hamster and frozen food.

Caption tells story in one sentence.

Prose under photo.

The Sun

B

Hamster that nearly had its chips

Pet's narrow squeak in freezer is a puzzle for scientists, report **Tracy Connor** and **Nigel Hawkes**

Headline large but less eye-catching.

Large close-up **photo** of hamster.

No **caption** – photo and prose tell the story.

Prose wraps around photo.

The Times

Advertisements

- You need a clear picture of what job a text is trying to do. Then you look at its details and decide how well it is doing that job.

- The layout of a text is important. Different layouts give different messages.

See page 6

5 Read the advertisement opposite. Use HIP to find your way around it quickly. Then work out what job it is trying to do.

The advertisement is about …
It is written for people who …
The writer wants the readers to …

See page 16

6 Read the text through carefully. Then copy out and complete this chart.

		Where is it on the page?	*What* does it make me notice?	*How* does it make me notice it?
H	**Heading**			
I	**Illustration**			
P	**Prose**	in a block at the bottom	the picture above	it's like a stage the picture stands on

7 Now write three paragraphs explaining how well the advertisement does its job. Use your answers to question 6 to help you.

Paragraph 1   The heading is effective because it says … It is … It makes the audience notice … which is important because … You notice this because …

Paragraph 2   The illustration is eye-catching and … It shows you … It makes you …

Paragraph 3   The prose …

WANTED!

Adventurous people throughout the UK to do something like this …

for FREE!

Help us raise funds by making an exciting 10,000 feet, freefall parachute jump. If you raise the minimum amount of money, you will get to jump for FREE! You don't even need to have done anything like this before.

For a free information pack call

0171 833 9549

This event is organised to raise money for ChildHope to help street children worldwide.

ChildHope, Lector Court, 151 Farringdon Road, London EC1R 3AF

Registered Charity No. 328434

Questions

Find out how well you have understood this unit by answering the questions below. First read the newspaper article opposite.

See page 16

1   Copy out and complete the chart below.

		Where is it on the page?	*What* does it make me notice?	*How* does it make me notice it?
H	Heading			
I	Illustration			
P	Prose			

2   Now read the prose carefully and look back at your chart. Which statement below best describes the job the text is trying to do?

a   The writer wants you to think that what the actor did was awful. The writer also wants you to think that the police were silly to stop the actor's car.

b   The writer wants you to be amused that the actor was stopped on his way to rehearsals. The writer also wants you to think about going to see the play.

3   Now write three paragraphs about how well the text is doing its job. The ideas below may help you to get started.

The **h**eading is … I think the heading does … because the print is … and … the words …

The **i**llustration is a photograph showing … It is eye-catching because …

The **p**rose tells … It also tells you about the play … In the prose, it …

Actor's excuse when cops stopped him driving with a coffin on his car

I'M RE-HEARSE-ING

Shocked police officers pulled over a motorist because a coffin was wobbling on the roof of his car.

Members of the public had called the police to complain. They were outraged that the driver was not showing proper respect to the dead.

But motorist Theo Van Dot is no fiend. He is just an actor who was taking some props to rehearsals.

Mr Van Dot is playing the part of an undertaker called Dennis in a play called *Loot* written by Joe Orton. The play is on at Hampton Wick's Theatre next week.

The actor had collected the fake coffin from the drama department at Brooklands College, in Weybridge.

The play's director Patrick Wilde said: 'The coffin looks very real. It is amazing because something just like this happens in the play. A man carries money from a bank robbery around in his mother's coffin.'

When Theo arrived at rehearsals, he had problems making the rest of the cast believe that he was telling the truth about his brush with the law.

He said, 'No one believed me. I had to swear that it was true. I was embarrassed when the police stopped me. The officer started to laugh when he got closer to the car because he could tell the coffin was not real. I asked him if he wanted to look inside, but he refused.'

Adapted from *The Kingston Informer*

A4 Reading leaflets and advertisements

When you are trying to understand what job an advertisement or leaflet is doing, ask yourself:

- **What** is being 'sold'? This is the (p)roduct – it can be goods or an idea.

- **Who** does the advertiser want to persuade? This is the (a)udience.

1 Read the texts opposite. Copy out and complete the chart below.

   a Work out what each product is.

   b Then decide who the writer is trying to persuade.

   c Give a reason for your choice of audience.

Advertisement	Product	Audience	Reason
A		People who want a really cheap ...	It offers ...
B		People who have ... but have not yet ...	
C	Treatment which will ...		
D	The chance to ...		

Advertisements

A

£11.99
LINE RENTAL
& free
CONNECTION

CALLS FROM ONLY 2P PER MIN

The Nokia 5110 is the mobile phone that everyone is talking about. Connect today and it can be yours – for free!

- **Free Nokia 5110 digital phone** worth £19.99
- **Free Connection worth £35**
- **Free calls – 200 minutes per** month worth up to £120 per year
- **Free Portable hands-free kit** worth up to £30
- **Free Carry case, in-car adaptor** and holder worth up to £60
- **Free Local Call Option** worth £15
- **Free Next Day Delivery**

All of this, and your line rental is just £11.99 a month!

Call KJC now on freephone
0800 959999

B

Helping you to get online.

Tesconet now offers free unlimited Internet access to all Clubcard members! Packs are available in-store or you can register online.

- Unlimited free Internet access (cost of local calls excluded)
- Five free e-mail addresses
- 10mb free webspace
- Jargon-free help

Pick up a connection pack in-store or visit the Tesco website at www.tesco.co.uk

C

REGROW

John Hartson
Premier League Footballer

12 months ago   TODAY

REPLACE

Graham Gooch
English cricket selector

3 years ago   TODAY

RING NOW

No one needs to suffer from hair loss. *ADVANCED* Laser Therapy helps to regrow your own hair. Strand-by-Strand replaces lost hair. No surgery is needed! So to regrow or replace your hair, ring Advanced Hair Studio today. Studios all over the UK

Name _____
Address _____
_____
Tel: _____

ADVANCED Hair Studio®
London · Brussels · Tokyo
Melbourne · Hong Kong

0845 600 8899
Carlton House, 46–50 Chertsey Road, West Byfleet, Surrey KT14 7AN

D

A NEW LIFE ABROAD!

If you're looking for a change, how about living and working in a different country?

Whatever your background, First Point can get you that new life abroad. We can help you get your visa and we will give you all the practical support you're likely to need.

Take your first step towards a brand new future. Call or write for our Information Pack today. Quote reference: BIG

FIRST POINT
INTERNATIONAL

York House, 17 Great Cumberland Place, London W1H 7LA

☎ **0171 724 9669** **24** HOURS

2 Now read the texts opposite. What is the product in each one?

In advertisement A, the product is …

3 Decide what the purpose of the leaflet is.

4 Choose the right audience below for each of the advertisements opposite. Give reasons for your answer.

See page 24

a	**b**	**c**	**d**

Now you can tell *what* the product is, and *who* it is for. Next look at *how* the advertisement tries to persuade the reader to have the product. Ask yourself:

- **How** is the reader persuaded?
  This is the **m**essage – what you are told
  that makes the product sound good:
  It's good value.

- **Why** will the audience be persuaded
  by the message? This is the **a**ppeal:
  They want a bargain.

5 Look at each advertisement. Choose the sentence halves below that give the **message** it is telling its readers.

This product is	service at a reasonable price.
This product is a very high-quality	you change the way you look.
This product will make you	the best value for money.
This product can help	more attractive to the opposite sex.

The message of advertisement A is that this product …

6 Read each advertisement in turn. Then note a reason why the audience would be persuaded by each advertisement's message. (This is the advertisement's **appeal**.)

A person who wanted to get rid of their tattoos would be persuaded by advertisement A because …

A

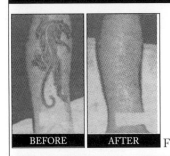

Tattoo Removal

- Free consultation
- Available Nationwide
- Registered with the Local Health Authority
- No Surgery

THE **LASER CLINIC**

FREEPHONE NOW FOR LEAFLET & DETAILS

BEFORE   AFTER

0800 227777

B

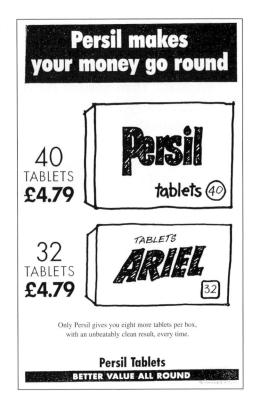

Persil makes your money go round

40 TABLETS **£4.79**

Persil tablets 40

32 TABLETS **£4.79**

TABLETS ARIEL 32

Only Persil gives you eight more tablets per box, with an unbeatably clean result, every time.

Persil Tablets

BETTER VALUE ALL ROUND

C

ADVERTISEMENT

LIAM'S THE **COOLEST** BOY IN THE SCHOOL. BUT MY BRACES FEEL SO **SLIMY**, I KNOW HE WON'T BE INTERESTED.

BRACE MATE

BRACEMATE TO THE RESCUE! BRACEMATE KILLS PLAQUE, KEEPS YOUR BRACE **TINGLINGLY** CLEAN AND HELPS KEEP YOUR BREATH REALLY **FRESH**.

3M

WOW! THANKS BRACEMATE - NOW I KNOW JUST HOW GOOD LIAM'S KISSES ARE!

BRACEMATE™ is only suitable for removable braces and retainers

D

red DRIVING SCHOOL LTD

NEW Air-Conditioned mk2 Renault Clios

- From a FULL hour to an intensive course
- Discounts for block bookings
- FREE local pick up – from home, school or work
- Punctual and reliable with no car sharing
- Initial assessment, theory training and mock tests
- Post test and motorway training

First 5 Lessons ONLY **£50**

FREEPHONE red on:

08000 180 171

Questions

Find out how well you have understood the work in this unit. First read the leaflet opposite. Then answer the questions below.

Product

Audience

See page 24

Message

Appeal

See page 26

1 Which of the products below is the leaflet trying to make you aware of?

a How to become a model.

b A makeover and photographic session.

c How to change the way you look.

2 Who is the audience the leaflet is hoping to reach? How do you know?

The leaflet is hoping to reach … You can tell because it says … and the illustrations show …

3 Explain what message the leaflet gives you about a Covershots photographic shoot. Write a paragraph in your own words. The words in the box may help you.

| professional luxurious friendly stunning |

4 Why do you think this message would appeal to the leaflet's audience?

WIN a £500 portrait and makeover

Have you always wanted to see how good you can look?

This is your chance to show yourself (and the world!) that you too can look as glamorous as any top model. Experience the thrill of a professional photographic shoot and be transformed by Cover Shots International's make-up/styling artists and photographers in their luxurious and friendly city centre studios. **Let them create the looks you've always wanted.**

THE PHOTOGRAPHS ARE STUNNING –
you may well want to buy enlargements. However, there is no obligation to do so.

HUNDREDS OF PRIZES
- First prize is a free session and a framed portrait – total value £500.
- Hundreds of runners-up prizes of a free session involving more than two hours of photographic makeover, hairstyling, photo shoot and same day viewing of your pictures (photographs not included) – value £150.

HOW TO ENTER
To enter this fabulous prize draw, simply answer the questions on this card (for research purposes only) and post the whole completed entry card in the post – no stamp required – **It's as simple as that. Good luck!**

Which film starred Julia Roberts?

A ☐ Fatal Attraction   B ☐ Grease

C ☐ Pretty Woman   D ☐ The Piano

Why would you particularly like to win a Cover Shots session?

E ☐ I could never afford it otherwise

F ☐ Because I'm not getting any younger

G ☐ I'd pay anything for a good picture of myself

H ☐ I want to give it to someone I love

If you win a prize, which studio would you go to?

I ☐ London   K ☐ Birmingham

L ☐ Manchester   M ☐ Glasgow

If you are lucky enough to win a prize, what is the best hour of the day to telephone you?

N ☐ before noon   P ☐ 12 noon – 3 pm

Q ☐ 3 pm – 6 pm   R ☐ 6 pm – 7.30 pm

S ☐ 7.30 pm – 10 pm

Age

T ☐ Under 18   V ☐ 18–30

W ☐ 31–40   X ☐ 41–50

Y ☐ over 50

A5 Looking at details

Details are important because they give you more information.

First decide what job the details are doing. Details might:

- help you to notice differences – *between a healthy person and a sick one*

- create an impression or picture – *that someone is feeling happy or sad*

- persuade you to choose one product rather than another – *to buy a particular make of mobile phone.*

Then decide how each detail helps do that job.

Passage
Questions
Re-read
Search

Details can help you notice differences

1   Read passage A opposite. Then study the pictures at the bottom of the page. Which picture shows Dudley? Use details from the text to explain why you are right.

2   Read passage B opposite. Which picture shows Harry?

3   Use details to explain why the other pictures do not show Harry.

Picture … could not be Harry because the text says that Harry … and the boy in the picture has …

4   Now think about what the details tell you about Dudley and Harry. Which boy do you find more interesting? Give four reasons for your choice.

I think … is a more interesting character than … The text says …

A

Dudley

Dudley had a large pink face, not much neck, small watery blue eyes and thick blond hair that lay smoothly on his thick fat head. Harry's Aunt often said that Dudley looked like a baby angel. Harry often said that Dudley looked like a pig in a wig.

5   Dudley was counting his birthday presents. His face fell.

'Thirty-six,' he said, looking up at his mother and father. 'That's two less than last year.'

Harry, who could see a huge Dudley tantrum coming on, began wolfing down his bacon as fast as possible in case Dudley turned the table over.

B

Harry

Perhaps it had something to do with sleeping in a dark cupboard, but Harry had always been small and skinny for his age. He looked even smaller and skinnier than he really was because all he had to wear were old clothes of Dudley's and Dudley was about four times bigger

5   than he was. Harry had a thin face, knobbly knees, black hair and bright-green eyes. He wore round glasses held together with a lot of Sellotape because of all the times Dudley had punched him on the nose. The only thing Harry liked about his own appearance was a very thin scar on his forehead which was shaped like a bolt of

10   lightning. He had had it as long as he could remember and the first question he could ever remember asking his aunt was how he had got it.

'In the car crash when your parents died,' she had said, 'And don't ask questions.'

Adapted from *Harry Potter and the Philosopher's Stone*
by J. K. Rowling

A

B

C

D

Details can help to create a picture or impression

1 Read the passage opposite. The details create a picture of Johnny's hairstyle.

2 Copy out and complete the chart below. Find four details to go in each column.

What Johnny's hair *looks like*	What *Johnny did*
1 a crusty, rebel grunge look (lines 3–4)	let it grow …
2 … (lines 6–7)	
3	
4	

3 Look at the details in the first column of your chart. Explain what impression each detail creates. The words below should help you get started.

   a The words … suggest that Johnny thinks that he has made his hair look …

   b … makes it sound as if his hair is made up of bits of dirty animals.

   c The words 'racehorse's blanket after …' make you think about just how sweaty and smelly it must be because a … running …

   d … shows that the grease in his hair is so solid it …

4 Now look at the details in the second column of your chart. Write a sentence explaining how each detail helps you picture how Johnny's hair looks now.

> The words 'let it grow' suggest Johnny's hair is … and out of …

Johnny's good hair day

I had to look cool when I appeared in the playground. I had to make a **dynamic** first impression on the new girls.

5   For once, styling my sacred hair took no time at all. I'd been developing a crusty, rebel, grunge look over the holidays. I'd been letting it grow out and not washing or combing it since 15th July. And I'd been rubbing John Innes Potting Compost No. 1 into the roots once a
10 week. The fringe hung limply over my eyes like a rack of rats' tails. The sides curled naturally behind my ears after weeks of flicking and the clump at the back swung greasily over my collar like a racehorse's blanket after a sweaty,
15 five mile chase. If I shook my head, lumps of oily **lard** sprayed the mirror. I was well pleased. It looked dead nasty.

Adapted from
The Changing Face of Johnny Casanova
by Jamie Rix

dynamic: *informal word meaning that he wants the girls to think he is wonderful*
lard: *white fat used in cooking*

Details can persuade you

1   FABSALES advertising company have been asked to write a magazine advertisement. It is to persuade teenagers to buy a new chocolate bar called *Winner*. Read their ideas opposite.

2   Choose three pieces of information from **A** that FABSALES should use in their advertisement for teenagers. Explain how they will help sell *Winner*.

3   Read what teenagers said about *Winner* in **B**. Choose two quotations for FABSALES to use in their advertisement. Explain why you chose them.

4   Choose two pieces of information from **A** and two views from **B** that FABSALES should *not* use in their advertisement for teenagers. Explain why they should not use them.

5   Which photograph should FABSALES use? Give reasons for your choice.

6   Read the text below. FABSALES are thinking of using it in their advertisement. Which details would you change to make it more persuasive? Write out your new version of the text.

Be One of Life's Winners ... enjoy a delicious success!

A short, satisfying bar. **Winner** knows how to keep you winning because it's only 200 calories (and there are no nasty additives or artificial colours in it either). It's really sweet and filling, too – you won't want any dinner after eating one of these!

Healthy, delicious ... and only 25p
... other chocolate is for losers!

FABSALES ideas for advertising the *Winner* chocolate bar

A   Important information about *Winner*

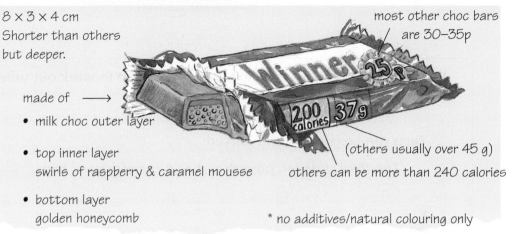

8 × 3 × 4 cm
Shorter than others
but deeper.

most other choc bars
are 30–35p

made of ⟶

- milk choc outer layer

- top inner layer
  swirls of raspberry & caramel mousse

- bottom layer
  golden honeycomb

200 calories   37 g

(others usually over 45 g)

others can be more than 240 calories

* no additives/natural colouring only

B   What teenagers said about *Winner* in taste tests

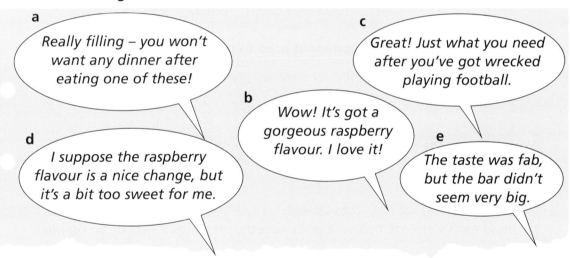

a
Really filling – you won't want any dinner after eating one of these!

c
Great! Just what you need after you've got wrecked playing football.

b
Wow! It's got a gorgeous raspberry flavour. I love it!

d
I suppose the raspberry flavour is a nice change, but it's a bit too sweet for me.

e
The taste was fab, but the bar didn't seem very big.

C   Photograph ideas

A6 *Is that a fact?*

When you spot a detail in a text, you often need to work out whether it is a fact or an opinion.

> **Facts** can be checked and proved:
>
> *The thief stole ten pounds out of Richard's sports bag.*

> **Opinions** are what someone believes:
>
> *He shouldn't have hidden the money in his bag.*

Sometimes a **fact** or an **opinion** is used to **persuade** you.

Work through the rest of this unit and see whether you can catch a thief!

1 Read each sentence below. Decide whether it states a fact or an opinion.

a Richard shoved his sports bag under the table while he ate his lunch.

b He had five £10 notes hidden under his kit.

c It was stupid to bring so much money to school.

d Richard had a games lesson at 3.00 pm.

e 'Richard, you've lost your kit on purpose.'

f Richard found his bag again but ten pounds was missing.

2 Mr Drake, the Head of Year 9, interviewed Richard about the theft. Read what Richard said.

> *I didn't tell anyone how much money I had on me, or where it was. I thought the money would be safer in my sports bag than in my wallet. I'd be stupid to walk around here with my wallet stuffed with £10 notes. That would be asking for it to get nicked!*
>
> *I had lunch with Paul, Asif and Dec. They're my friends, none of them would steal off me. It must be someone else.*
>
> *I haven't seen them since lunch time. I must have left my bag under the table in the dining room when we went off to registration.*
>
> *My dad will kill me if I don't get it back!*

3 Copy out and complete the chart below. Sort the information Richard gives Mr Drake into facts and opinions. Find at least three facts and six opinions.

Facts Richard tells Mr Drake	Richard's opinions
Richard had told no one how much money he had on him.	He thought the money was safer in his bag than in his wallet.
Richard had not told anyone where …	

Finding the thief

4 Read the script opposite. It is the conversation Richard and his friends had at lunch time before the money was stolen.

See page 10

5 Read each statement below. Write down one fact and one opinion from the passage to show that it is true.

a It's better to go into town and meet Stoney and his mates than go to Jo's party.

> Fact: Stoney and his mates are going to watch the football.
>
> Opinion: Stoney's always good for a laugh.

b It would be better to go to Jo's party (lines 1–9).

c Dec could do with some new clothes (lines 10–15).

d Paul is not mean (lines 14–17).

6 Look at the cartoon below. Then answer the questions.

> Richard thinks he's had some money stolen from his sports bag. What do you think might have happened to it?

> Asif: I reckon someone nicked it out of his wallet during games

> Paul: I think he might have left his bag behind somewhere after registration. Someone could have got to his wallet.

> Dec: Richard is useless at Maths. He probably thought he had fifty quid but there was only ever forty.

a Who is most likely to be the thief? Why?

b What does each of the other boys say that shows he is unlikely to be the thief?

… is unlikely to be the thief because …

Richard is having lunch with Paul, Asif and Dec in the school canteen.

Asif	I'm not going to Jo's party. It'll be really boring. Let's go into town with Stoney and his mates. They're going to watch the football. Stoney's always good for a laugh.
Paul	Now that *is* boring! You want me to waste £10 I haven't got watching Tonton lose another match when I could be at a free party. I don't think so! Go on, Asif. Come to the party with us. It'll be fun.
Dec	Only if Jo's younger brother isn't there with his friends.
Asif	Well, he's bound to be. So I'm not going.
Dec	What are you going to wear? I've got nothing. My trainers must be the least cool in the universe! They're really hideous!
Paul	You sound just like my sister!
Asif	Leave him alone. You know he's broke.
Paul	Not as broke as you are. You still owe me for that CD.
Asif	I said I'd give you the money next week. Don't be so mean!
Paul	I'm not mean. I lent you £10 and now I need it back.
Dec	Ask Richard to lend you some. He's always loaded.
Richard	Funny!
Paul	Well, you are. I bet you're going shopping tonight for something to wear to Jo's party.
Richard	Well, I …
Paul	Told you!
Richard	What do you need the money for?
Paul	I just need it. So Asif had better give it back to me, or else …

Sound of school bell. They go off squabbling. Richard's bag is left behind.

Facts and opinions can be used to persuade you

1   Read the text opposite. The writer has used a mixture of facts and opinions to persuade students to take good care of their money in school.

2   Read lines 1–6. Find three worrying facts about what happened to students' money last year.

3   Read lines 7–16.

   a   What is the writer's opinion of people who:

      i   don't bring money to school?

      ii   bring in cheques to pay for school trips?

   b   Which fact makes writing cheques a good way to keep money safe?

4   Read lines 17–32.

   a   Pick out three of the writer's opinions which might persuade students to think carefully about how to handle their money.

   > The writer says only …

   b   How has the writer used facts and opinions to persuade students of ways to keep their money safe?`

   > First the writer tells students some worrying … This makes you think …
   >
   > The writer calls people who … This makes you think …
   >
   > The fact that cheques can only … makes you think …
   >
   > At the end of the leaflet the writer persuades students to handle their money wisely by saying …

KEEPING YOUR CASH SAFE

Did you know that last year St Martin's students 'lost' over £500? Only £100 was ever found again.

Did you know that most of the missing money went during lunch time? Most of the students did not notice it had gone until the end of the day.

Of course, there is one smart way to be sure you still have your money at the end of the school day … don't bring it to school in the first place! But if you *have* to bring money to school, follow this advice.

Money for trips

Be sensible. Ask your parents to write a cheque rather than sending you in with the cash. All cheques for school trips etc. should be made out to the school. Then, even if you lose the cheque, no one else can cash it. (Unless their name is St Martin's High School, of course!!)

Safe ways to keep your money

If you have to bring **more than £10** to school, the best thing is to hand it over to your Head of Year. They will seal it in an envelope and ask you to sign the envelope. Then it will be put in the school safe. When you sign the safe book at the end of the school day, the Head of Year can check your signature to make sure it really is you collecting it.

Any other money you have in school is safest if it's kept on you **all the time**. So put your wallet in your trouser or skirt pocket.

- Never leave money in your coat, in your bag, or anywhere that someone might be able to take it from without you seeing.
- Only fools boast about how much money they're carrying. After all, you never know who else is listening. (Don't stand there counting handfuls of it either!)
- Act smart – don't tell everyone you're going shopping after school and then list all the things you're going to buy. That will only tell a thief you might have a lot of money on you.

A7 Reading between the lines

> Readers are really detectives. They have to look at the clues a writer gives and work out what is really going on.
>
> Writers do not just *tell* you what is happening. Instead they **show** you events and let you work out what is going on.

1   Read texts **A** and **B**. Each is the beginning of a story. Which one *shows* you what is happening, and which one just *tells* you?

2   Read text **B**. Which details (clues) show you these pieces of information?

    a   The bomb landed last night (lines 1–5).

    b   The policeman gets on well with the soldiers (lines 6–17).

    c   The soldier does not expect the bomb to be stolen (lines 18–26).

    d   Someone is trying to steal the bomb (lines 27–29).

3   Read the questions in the box below. Then answer questions **a** and **b**.

> • What has happened to Paradise Street?
>
> • What has the weather been like?
>
> • Will the unexploded bomb go off?
>
> • Who is going to steal an unexploded bomb?

    a   Would a reader need to ask any of these questions after reading text **B**? Why?

    b   Which of these questions might a reader still ask after reading text **A**?

4   Which text is most likely to make a reader want to read on? Why?

A

It is during the Second World War. Yesterday Paradise Street, in Slate, was bombed. Tonight a policeman goes to the ruined street where the army is sorting out an unexploded bomb. He stops and has a friendly chat and a cup of tea and a sandwich with a soldier.
5   It is 2 a.m. and it is raining. The soldier does not expect anyone to steal the bomb. Then they hear the sound of Mrs Tachyon moving about. She knocks a brick down onto the bomb and it explodes.

B

Johnny and the bomb

The policeman turned the corner, and walked up the next street, his boots seeming very loud in the stillness.

The beat took him up as far as the Methodist chapel, and in theory would take him down Paradise Street, but it didn't do that tonight
5 because there was no Paradise Street any more. Not since last night.

There was a lorry parked by the chapel. Light leaked out from the **tarpaulin** that covered the back.

He banged on it.

'You can't park that 'ere, gents,' he said. 'I fine you one mug of tea
10 and we shall say no more about it, eh?'

The tarpaulin was pushed back and a soldier jumped out. There was a brief vision of the interior – a warm tent of orange light, with a few soldiers sitting around a little stove, and the air thick with cigarette smoke. The soldier grinned.

15 'Gi'us a mug and a wad for the sergeant,' he said, to someone in the lorry.

A tin mug of scalding black tea and a brick-thick sandwich were handed out.

'Much obliged,' said the policeman, taking them. He leaned against the lorry.

'How's it going then?' he said. 'Haven't heard a bang.'

'It's a 25-pounder,' said the soldier. 'Went right down through the
20 cellar floor. You lot took a real pounding last night, eh? Want a look?'

'Is it safe?'

'Course not,' said the soldier cheerfully. 'That's why we're here, right? Come on.' He pinched out his cigarette and put it behind his ear.

'I thought you lot'd be guarding it,' said the policeman.

25 'It's two in the morning and it's been pissing down,' said the soldier. 'Who's going to steal an unexploded bomb?'

'Yes, but …' The sergeant looked in the direction of the ruined street.

There was the sound of bricks sliding.

'Someone is, by the sound of it,' he said.

From *Johnny and the Bomb* by Terry Pratchett

tarpaulin: *a waterproof sheet*

Looking for clues

The details a writer puts in a text are *clues*. The reader is a detective. When you have worked out the clues, you can understand what is really going on.

These details ...	... give us a clue ...	... which suggests ...
A single tear slid from under Darren's tightly shut eyelids. It was joined by another, then another, until a small stream flowed down onto the fist cupping his chin.	Darren is crying hard.	Darren must be feeling very sad.

1   Read the passage opposite. Study the highlighted details 1–6. Then match each detail to the right clue (A–F) below.

    A Allison has planned this very carefully. A = 1

    B Allison is feeling nervous.

    C Allison is using information most people do not know.

    D Allison is worried she might not succeed.

    E Allison needs a weapon to do this.

    F Allison has done this so many times before that she is good at it and enjoys it.

2   Copy out and complete the table below. Fill in each detail from the text in the order 1 to 6. Write beside each detail the clue that you matched with it in question 1. In the third column explain what each clue suggests.

These details ...	... give us a clue ...	... which suggests ...
1 Four o'clock exactly. She's got nearly an hour to spare.	Allison has planned this very carefully. Allison is very early.	Being somewhere before five o'clock is important.
2 Allison knows ...		

3   Write a paragraph explaining what Allison might be going to do.

    I think Allison is ... because ... She is probably on her way to ...

The professional

1   Allison steps off the tube at Piccadilly Circus, then she looks at her watch. **Four o'clock exactly. She's got nearly an hour to spare.**

2   **Allison knows precisely what time to be there. She's got contacts, inside information.** But then Allison is a professional. Ought to be.

3   **Been doing it long enough, started nine years ago when she was eleven. Never stopped. Couldn't now if she wanted to. An addict and a professional.**

4   **Time for a coffee. Might steady her nerves.** For make no mistake, this is the big one. The one she's been waiting for. She stares at the dregs in the coffee cup. **What if she failed? No, impossible.**

5   No trouble about finding her way. Been there heaps of times. But today was the peak. No doubt about it.

6   **Allison decided to examine her weapons. A nervous habit. Always did it.** First she took out her most important weapon. Check it, that's the first rule.

**Adapted from *Touching Greatness*
by *Pete Johnson***

Questions

Find out how well you have understood the work in this unit. Read the text opposite. Then answer the questions below.

1   Read the text opposite again. This time, stop at the end of each paragraph and answer the questions below about the details in bold.

    a   What clue do these details give you?

        The first clue tells you that Callum is fascinated … even though …

    b   What does the clue suggest?

        The clue suggests that Callum feels …

2   Read these three possible suggestions of what Callum has done. Which one is the most likely? Use details in the text to show why you are right.

    a   Callum has committed a robbery.

    b   Callum has set fire to his home.

    c   Callum has run away from home.

3   Decide whether each of the statements below is true or false. Choose one detail from the text each time to prove you are right.

    a   Callum does not bother to hide.

    b   At first Callum is not sure if his plan has succeeded.

    c   The door is getting very hot.

    d   The author has made the fire seem as if it is alive.

    e   Callum feels sorry for what he has done.

4   Write one paragraph to answer each point below. Use your answers to the questions above to help you.

    a   Describe what Callum has done.

        Callum has …

    b   Explain how he feels about his crime.

        Callum feels … because …

    c   Explain how the writer has made the text interesting to read.

        It is interesting when …

Firebug

Callum crouched in the blackest shadows of the alley-way. **He was gazing intently at the front door of the house across the street. It was crazy to hang around here. He should have been running now**, putting as much distance between himself and his place as possible. But he just couldn't help staying to watch.

He had his jacket hood up so no one would recognise him. The drawstring was pulled tight, leaving only a small hole. All you could see was a cold white nose and two glittering eyes.

Nervously, Callum rattled the box of matches in his pocket.

Nothing was going to happen.

Yes, it was.

Behind the glass panels in the front door of the house there was a weird orange glow. It throbbed, like the windows of an alien spacecraft. The paint on the door was blistering. The blisters swelled, then popped like bubble gum.

Callum held his breath. In his eyes, which were almost all you could see of his face, was **a strange expression. It was a mixture of terror, excitement – and pride.**

Through the glass, Callum could see small flames now. They were racing upwards like squirrels up a tree. That was the blue curtain burning. The one that you pulled over the front door to keep the draughts out. **Callum knew about the curtain because his mother had made it last winter.**

Firebug by Susan Gates

A8 Reading poetry

> Reading poetry can be a bit like watching television. They both have:
>
> - words
> - sound effects
> - pictures.

Reading the words

Follow these three steps to find out *what a poem is saying.*

Step A	Read the poem aloud

When you read a poem aloud, you need to:

- pause at the end of each stanza.

- notice the **rhyming** words that end with the same sound, like *game* and *aim*. Make a short pause after each rhyming word.

- notice the *important* parts that you want to say strongly or slowly.

Copy the poem opposite out onto the centre of a clean page. Make notes around the poem showing how the poem should be read aloud. Put in as much expression as possible.

Jason's Trial

Jason was a football freak;

He really *loved* the game: ◄——— say 'loved' strongly

say it slowly to make it hit home ——► To be a *first-class footballer*

Was his *one* aim. ◄——— say 'one' stongly

Step B	Read one sentence at a time

Explain what each shows. Jason loved football. He played for … when he …

Step C	Decide what the poem is about

Now write a paragraph to say what the poem is about.

Jason wanted to … he trains … When he has his trial he … but he does not …

Jason's Trial

Jason was a football freak;
He really loved the game:
To be a first-class footballer
Was his one aim.

5 He practised every day and played
Again each night in dream;
When he was twelve they chose him for
The school's first team.

He was quite brilliant. Five years passed
10 And – though rarely this occurs –
It seemed his dreams might all come true:
He was given a trial by Spurs.

He played a blinder on the day;
The spectators cheered and roared,
15 And after the match he was asked to appear
Before the Selection Board.

The Chairman said, 'I've got the reports
From our experts who watched you play:
Your speed and ball-control were fine;
20 For tackling you get an A.

'And when our striker scored his goal
You were first to jump on his back,
And when *you* scored you punched the air
Before you resumed the attack.

25 'So far, so good; but you were weak
On the thing our lads do best;
It seems you hardly spat at all,
So you failed the spitting-test.

'But don't despair. If you go home
30 And practise every day
You still might learn to spit with style
In the true professional way.'

by Vernon Scannell

Reading a poem's sound effects

After you have worked out what a poem is about, listen to its sounds. Try to hear how they help to make the meaning clearer.

1   Listen for any **rhythms**.

   • Is the beat slow? Or is it fast, as in: *rockin' rollin' divin' slidin'* ?

   • Does it just sound like a conversation? Or like a chant as in: *I'm a shirt removin' crowd salutin' ...*?

   • Does it stay the same all the way through the poem or does it change?

2   Ask: **How does the rhythm suit the meaning of those lines**? *The rhythm in lines ... shows the striker's energy and excitement.*

3   Listen for **repeated words and sounds**:

   • Does it rhyme regularly or not? *The word at the end of each line always ends with **in'**, but most of the time they do not rhyme.*

   • Do words begin with the same letter (alliteration)? *s**houlder s**hruggin'*

   • Do any words sound like their meaning (onomatopoeia)? *buzz*

4   Ask yourself: **How does the sound effect I have noticed suit the meaning of these words?**

   The alliteration in:

   'shimmy shootin' shin spinnin' '

   makes these words roll together smoothly as you say them. It helps you think about how smoothly and skilfully the striker works the ball.

1   Read the poem opposite. Follow the steps you learned on page 48. Then explain what the poem is about.

   The poem is about a striker who has ... and is feeling ...

2   Now read the poem aloud. Listen for the *rhythm*. Which sentence below best describes what you can hear?

   A   A slow, regular beat making it sound sad.

   B   A fast, regular beat making it sound lively, as if the striker is excited.

3   Many of the words in the poem have the same beat and end in *in'* (*ing*). Which words best describe the feeling they give?

sad	happy	relaxed	excited	worried
bored	confident	triumphant	depressed	

When you read this poem, remember that the letter *g* is missing off the end of most of the words – *removin'* is really *removing*. The poet has done this to make the poem sound as if the striker is speaking.

Coolscorin' Matchwinnin' Celebratin' Striker!

I'm a shirt removin' crowd salutin'
handstandin' happy landin'
rockin' rollin' divin' slidin'
posin' poutin' loud shoutin'
5 pistol packin' smoke blowin'
flag wavin' kiss throwin'
hipswingin' armwavin'
breakdancin' cool ravin'
shoulder shruggin' team huggin'
10 hot shootin' rootin' tootin'
somersaultin' fence vaultin'
last minute goal grinnin'
shimmy shootin' shin spinnin'
celebratin' cup winnin' STRIKER!

by Paul Cookson

Reading a poem's pictures

Writers often use groups of words to make 'word pictures' or **images**. An image shows you what something is like. There are two main kinds of **imagery**.

1   In a **simile** two things are compared by saying they are *like* one another. The writer uses the words **as** or **like**.

   *The cat's fur was black **as** the darkest night.*
   *His eyes shone **like** a car's headlights.*

2   In a **metaphor** two things are compared by making the picture *without* using the words **as** or **like**. One thing *is* the other thing.

   *The cat's fur **was** a matted carpet.*

1   A poet is trying to describe a strange creature. Read the word pictures on the opposite page.

2   Find and list the six similes. Then find and list the three metaphors.

3   The poet wants the creature to seem really impressive. Choose the five images that you think describe the creature best.

   a   Copy and complete this chart. Explain what is being compared in each image.

Image	Feature being compared
skin glistens like oil	the glistening (shining) of the creature's skin is compared to the glistening of oil

   b   Explain how each image makes the creature seem impressive.

   When the writer compares ... with ... it makes the creature seem impressive because ...

A

The creature's black skin glistens like oil.

B

Its roar is thunder.

C

Its voice is like the roar of a waterfall.

D

The creature is as strong as a bulldozer.

E

Its hair is long twisted ropes hanging from its head.

F

Strands of saliva like droplets of glue dripped from its tongue.

G

Yellow fangs guard a mouth like a cave.

H

Its legs are as strong as stone pillars.

I

Its horns are two sharp daggers.

Questions

Find out how well you have understood the work in this unit. Read the poem opposite. Then answer the questions below.

1   Write a sentence explaining what the poem is about.

2   Is the poem meant to be serious or amusing (or both)? Give reasons for your answer.

3   Read the underlined phrases in the poem aloud. Choose a sound effect from the list for each phrase. Why does each sound effect suit that description?

   The phrase 'purr, puffing' uses … It suits the description because …

   • words beginning with the same sounds (*alliteration*)
   • regular rhythm
   • rhyme
   • repetition of words
   • words which sound like their meaning (*onomatopoeia*).

4   Look at lines 1, 11 and 13. What metaphor is the poet using all through the poem?

   The poet says that … are …

5   Now look at the phrases in bold in the poem. Each is a metaphor for a part of a car. Match each word picture to the correct label on the car opposite.

   'hard shelled monsters' is label … showing the bodywork of the car.

6   Copy out and complete the chart below. Show how each phrase in bold makes a comparison with a car. Then explain how it makes the car seem frightening.

Image	Comparison	How it makes the car seem frightening
hard shelled monsters	Car's bodywork is hard like a monster's shell	Having a hard shell means it can easily kill but is very hard to kill. This shows the monster is very powerful.
four huge round feet		

The Hedgehog Warns Her Children

Beware, my children, those **hard shelled monsters**
With the soft masters within,
For they will crush us if we cross their paths,
With their **four huge round feet**.

5 Sometimes they _purr, puffing dark clouds behind_,
Sometimes they <u>roar</u>,
Raking the sky with sharp rods of sound;
But <u>always they are savage</u>
<u>Always they are wild,</u>
10 And, each one of us, they would kill.

So, my children, beware the hard shelled monsters
With the soft masters within,
Beware the **monsters** called …
CAR.

by David R. Morgan

A9 Quoting from a text

> You are *quoting* when you use words from a text in your own writing. The boxes below show you how to set out quotations.

Quoting prose

1   Copy the words, spellings and punctuation in the quotation *exactly* from the original text.

2   You can write quotations of **one to three words** as part of a sentence like this:

quotation marks

The words 'his eye' tell you that there is something unusual about his eyes.

3   Quotations of **four or more words** must go on a new line.

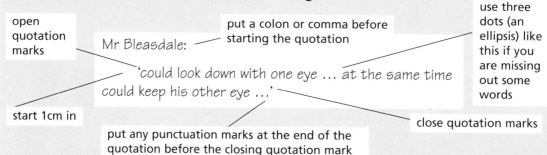

open quotation marks

put a colon or comma before starting the quotation

use three dots (an ellipsis) like this if you are missing out some words

Mr Bleasdale:

'could look down with one eye … at the same time could keep his other eye …'

start 1cm in

close quotation marks

put any punctuation marks at the end of the quotation before the closing quotation mark

Quoting poetry

If you are quoting from a poem, set it out so that it looks exactly the same as the original poem. Use the same line endings and beginnings.

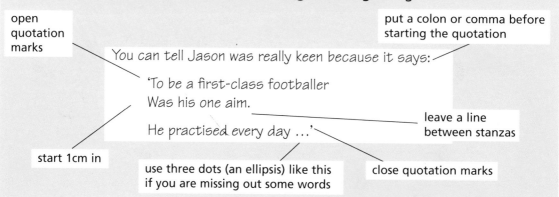

open quotation marks

put a colon or comma before starting the quotation

You can tell Jason was really keen because it says:

'To be a first-class footballer
Was his one aim.

He practised every day …'

leave a line between stanzas

start 1cm in

use three dots (an ellipsis) like this if you are missing out some words

close quotation marks

Read the passage below. Then answer the question using quotations. Make sure you set out the quotations correctly.

> The first time I ever saw Mr Bleasdale take the register, I couldn't take my eyes off him. That was because he didn't take his eye off me. Yes – his eye. His left eye.

1   Which words show that the writer thinks there is something strange about Mr Bleasdale?

The words … and … show that …

Don't just copy out large chunks of text. Only quote the words that you need to make your point.

How do you know the writer remembered Mr Bleasdale clearly?

The writer says it was Mr Bleasdale's 'left eye' which was fixed on him. The fact that he can tell you which eye it was, shows he remembers the teacher clearly.

2   Read the text below. Then use a short quotation to help you answer each question that follows. Make sure you explain how the words you choose answer the question.

> It was on my first day at Grammar School and I'd never seen anything like it. I'd been put in 1B and Mr Bleasdale was our form master. He also taught Latin and he could look down with one eye to read, write or take the register and at the same time could keep his
> 5   other eye on the class. And it never blinked. It just stared at us making sure nobody misbehaved while he was calling our names.

a   How do you know this is the first time the writer has met Mr Bleasdale?

   It was the writer's:
      'first day at Grammar School'.

b   What is amazing about Mr Bleasdale?

c   Could Mr Bleasdale have a false eye?

A10 *I can't understand this bit …*

> Everyone has to read words or sentences they don't understand. But do you know what to do when that happens? Work through this unit and get to grips with some great tips to help you cope.

Use a dictionary when you can

 Remember

- The words in a dictionary are arranged in **alphabetical order**: *A B C …*

  Then they are listed in alphabetical order of the next letter in the word. Because all the words below begin with C, they are listed in the alphabetical order of their *second* letters:

  car
  certain
  cinema
  cord
  curtain

- A word may have **more than one meaning**. Work out which meaning is the one you need by looking at how the word works in the rest of the sentence.

1   Read each of the sentences below. Use a dictionary to help you find out what each word in bold means.

   a   Don't just **fritter** your money away on sweets and magazines.

   b   Police were called in to **quell** a riot.

   c   Paul thought the party was **abysmal**.

   d   Our new toothpaste has been **accredited** by British dentists.

   e   The house was very **ostentatious**.

2   Now write a sentence explaining each word in your own words.

   If you fritter your money, it means you …

Use the rest of the text to help you understand a difficult word

No dictionary? Don't despair. Use the clues in the rest of the text to help you guess the meaning of any difficult words.

Ask yourself these three questions:

1 What is the whole paragraph about?

2 What is the sentence containing the word about?

3 What should the word mean to make sense in that sentence?

1 Read the paragraph below. Then answer the three questions.

Ricky crept into the hallway. Good, his dad must be asleep. The landing light was off. If he could just **ascend** the stairs to his bedroom without making a noise, then perhaps in the morning he could lie about what time he got in.

a What is the whole paragraph about?

b What is the sentence containing the word in **bold** about?

c What should the word mean if it is going to make sense in that sentence?

2 Read each text below. Work out what the word in bold means. Then answer the question on the meaning of the paragraph.

A

Police records show that there have been fifteen fights outside Volts nightclub during the last two months. All of them involved young men aged between 16 and 21. It's no wonder that Volts is becoming **notorious**.

a What kind of reputation is Volts nightclub getting?

'notorious' means something like … so the kind of reputation …

B

Lynne Zenman is the youngest British player to reach the quarter finals at Wimbledon. She **ascribes** her success to her coach.

'Without Ali's help I wouldn't be here. He's really fussy about how I train and what I eat.'

b Why does Lynne think she is successful?

'ascribes' means something like … so Lynne thinks she is successful because …

Do you know the meaning of part of the word?

Longer words can be broken into parts:

unlikely = *un* + *like* + *ly*

| A **prefix** may have been added to the front to change the meaning | The main part is the word **root** | A **suffix** may have been added to the end to change the way the word can be used |

First work out the meaning of each part. Then you can have a good guess at what the whole word means.

1   Study the chart below. It shows the meaning of some prefixes. Use it to help you work out the meaning of the words in the sentences below.

Prefix	dis	mis	pre	re	un
Meaning	opposite/not	wrong	before	again	not

a   Helping the prisoner to escape would be **misguided**.

b   Our letters are being **redirected** for the next month.

c   It is **unthinkable** to tell lies about a friend.

d   The film is **pre-recorded** onto the video-tape.

e   Mum was very **displeased** with Keri for coming home late.

Do you know other members of the word family?

Sometimes you can see that a word belongs to the same family as another word that you understand. This can help you to guess its meaning.

decorate   decorator

decorative?

decorate   decorated

What do I do if the whole sentence is a problem?

1 Work out roughly what that sentence might be about by looking at the rest of the paragraph.

2 Try rearranging the sentence. You may understand each word but be confused by the way the sentence is organised.

You can often treat pairs of commas as if they are brackets around extra pieces of information.

Tariq, who was Abdul's brother, knew Lally was lying and he reckoned he knew, or thought he knew, why.

- **Read the main part of the sentence first:**

Tariq knew Lally was lying and he reckoned he knew why.

- **Then make sense of the extra bits of information:**

Tariq is Abdul's brother.

Tariq only thought he knew why.

1 Rearrange these sentences into one main part and two extra pieces of information.

a Barry knew that Arran, who had scored the winning goal, was waiting for Jim, the team's manager, to congratulate him.

b Thursday, which is the day after tomorrow, is Barry's (older) brother Mo's birthday.

c Arran's house is halfway between the chip shop, which you can smell a mile away, and the bus stop, where you can catch the number 45.

d No one, and that includes the writers of this book, understands every word or sentence, especially the more complicated ones, in an encyclopedia.

e If you follow all the good advice in this unit, which helps you understand difficult words, and learn all the tips in the other units (of course), then you will do really well in your exams.

B1 Gone fishing!

> Read the passage below. Lucas thinks he has caught a fish, but his dad thinks the line is hooked on the bottom. Lucas is about to prove his dad wrong …
>
> You are going to answer the question:
>
> How does the writer make this passage interesting and entertaining?

The Whopper

'That can't be a fish,' says Dad. 'You're snagged on the bottom.'

He is wrong. I know it is a fish because it is pulling the line out. Snags don't pull on the line.

My rod starts to bend and the line goes whizzing out.
5 Whatever it is, I know one thing. I have hooked a whopper.

'You're right, it is a fish,' yells Dad. 'And it's a big one. Give me the rod, Lucas, you might lose it.'

'I can land it,' I shout firmly. 'I know I can.'

For the next hour I play my fish. Sometimes he runs deep and
10 fast and the reel screeches like a cooked cat. Sometimes I almost get it to the edge of our boat and then it goes off again.

In the end I win. I get the fish to the edge of the boat and Dad pulls him in. I am grinning from ear to ear because I have landed him.

'It's only a shark,' says Dad with a bit of a grin. 'A small shark.
15 Not much good for eating. You might as well throw him back.'

'No way,' I say. 'You can eat shark.'

'All right,' says Dad, 'but you have to clean it. You caught it, you
clean it.'

Dad goes down the steps into the little cabin and leaves me up top.
20 I get out my cleaning knife and make a long slit in the shark's belly.
I throw the innards and other stuff overboard. Seagulls swoop around
fighting for the bits.

Finally I decide to look in the shark's stomach to see what it has
been eating. This will give me some clues as to what to use for bait.
25 I throw out some fish heads and shells. Then I see something a bit
different. I pick up this white, shrivelled thing. For about ten seconds
I stare at it. My mind goes numb and I can't quite make sense of what
I am seeing. I notice first of all that it has a fingernail. And a ring. Just
below the ring is a small tattoo of a bear. An angry bear.

30 It is a finger. I have just taken a human finger out of the shark's
stomach.

Adapted from *Uncanny* *by Paul Jennings*

What's it all about?

1 Read the passage again. Then read each statement below. Say whether it is true or false.

   a Lucas 'plays the fish' for an hour before catching it.

   b Dad wants Lucas to catch the fish on his own.

   c Lucas cuts open the shark's stomach to find ideas for bait.

 ## Looking at the detail

How Lucas and Dad get on

2 What does Dad think about Lucas's fish? (line 1)

3 What does Dad say when he realises it is a fish? (lines 6–7)

4 What does Dad say about the catch and why does he give a bit of a grin? (lines 14–15)

Entertaining descriptions

5 What image is used to describe the sound of the reel? (line 10)

6 What words tell you how Lucas feels when he lands the catch? (line 13)

7 What do the seagulls do when Lucas throws the innards into the sea? (lines 21–22)

A surprise ending

8 What three details tell you that Lucas is shocked by what he has found? (lines 26–28)

9 What two things make Lucas certain about what he has found? (line 28)

? The big question

10 How does the writer make this passage interesting and entertaining?

Use your answers to the questions on the opposite page to help you.

- The writer makes you want Lucas to catch the fish when Dad says … (line 1). When Lucas manages to … (lines 12–13), you feel really …

- The reader is entertained by how Lucas and his dad get on when … (lines 6–8) When Lucas catches the fish, Dad says …, but he gives … (lines 14–15).

- The writer uses images such as … (line 10) to make the passage more …

- When Lucas cuts the shark open, the reader is entertained by the description of … (lines 21–22).

- The surprise ending shocks the reader when Lucas finds … You can tell that Lucas is shocked because … The writer gives details like … and … before telling you that … (lines 23–31). This helps to make the passage …

B2 Death on a ferry

Read the passage opposite. On 7 March 1987, a car ferry called the Herald of Free Enterprise capsized (overturned) and 188 people died. Stephen Homewood remembers his feelings of horror.

You are going to answer the question:

How does the writer show the horror of the ferry disaster?

It's a nightmare!

The pens and pencils rolled first. Next papers, books and trays slid onto the floor. Then video-tapes crashed down and chairs fell over. And then there were screams, awful screams. I shall never forget them.

5   It had all started when the ship rolled. It was as if it swerved to miss something, then went straight again. But then it rolled back and this time it started to capsize. People were crying out in terror, and from that moment it seemed to be happening in slow motion.

10   All around me was horror. I clung to the wall to stop falling over. A woman in a wheelchair came sliding past my office. She had a look of total disbelief on her face. It said, 'This can't be happening to me, someone pinch me, it's a nightmare.' Later, I saw a body brought out of the
15 ship which I am sure was hers.

    I could see the bar. Men and women had been cheerfully drinking there only seconds ago. Now it was madness. Glasses and bottles were smashing, and trays smashing, and trays falling. Men, women and children
20 were grabbing hold of anything to hang on to. They screamed in terror at the tops of their voices because what was happening seemed unbelievable and impossible.

    The ferry's lights were still on. I could see people falling with such speed that when they hit the large glass

25 windows at the side of the ship, they left smears of blood. I was reminded horribly of insects and the marks they make when they hit a car windscreen.

Then sea water put out the ship's lights and we were in terrifying
30 darkness. From the first roll of the ship, the whole thing had lasted less than a minute. My first thought was about my son, Simon. I thought, 'I want to see Simon again'.

Adapted from
Zeebrugge: A Hero's Story
by Stephen Homewood
(with Stuart White)

1 Read lines 1–7. What happens on the ship?

2 Read lines 8–22. What happens to the people on the ship?

3 Read lines 23–27. What does the writer see and what does it remind him of?

4 Read lines 28–34. What happened on the ship and what did the writer think about?

Looking at the detail

5 Copy out the thought bubbles below about the disaster. Write down words from the passage that match each thought.

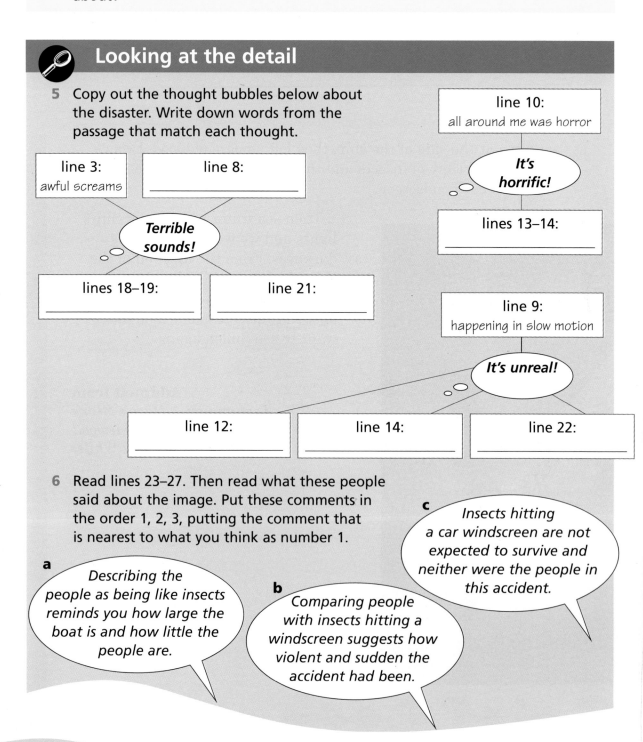

line 3:
awful screams

line 8:
_____

Terrible sounds!

lines 18–19:
_____

line 21:
_____

line 10:
all around me was horror

It's horrific!

lines 13–14:
_____

line 9:
happening in slow motion

It's unreal!

line 12:
_____

line 14:
_____

line 22:
_____

6 Read lines 23–27. Then read what these people said about the image. Put these comments in the order 1, 2, 3, putting the comment that is nearest to what you think as number 1.

a Describing the people as being like insects reminds you how large the boat is and how little the people are.

b Comparing people with insects hitting a windscreen suggests how violent and sudden the accident had been.

c Insects hitting a car windscreen are not expected to survive and neither were the people in this accident.

? The big question

7 **How does the writer show the horror of the ferry disaster?**

Use your answers to the above questions to help you.

- When the ship starts to sink, things ...

- The writer says he hears ...

- The writer gets across the horror by saying ...

- The horror seems unreal when the writer says ...

- The writer compares people to ... which makes me feel ...

- The final terror is when the lights ... and the writer thinks ...

- I feel the most powerful parts of his descriptions ... because ...

Key points

- Break down a passage into bits that you can manage. See how it is broken into sections. It is fairly simple here: there are six paragraphs. You cannot read everything at once, so simply take it a paragraph at a time.

- You can break questions down into smaller parts, too. Look how this unit does it for you for the big question. Once something is broken into smaller sections, it is much less of a problem.

- Make notes about what you read as you go. Then you don't have to trust your memory!

- In examinations and tests, you can underline or highlight parts of a passage. This helps you to find the parts you want to use.

B3 Shot down!

> Read the following passage. It is set during the Second World War. Two boys, Eric and Albert, hear a fighter aircraft crash and go to find it.
>
> You are going to answer the question:
>
> How does the writer build up tension in this passage?

The pilot

Then we began to hear the machine-guns up in the clouds; they sounded like a boy running a stick along a row of iron railings. Only lots of boys, and lots of railings.

'Goin' out for a look,' said Albert.

5   But he never did. Because at that moment we heard the engines. Howling, screaming. Coming straight at us like the end of the world. Louder and louder and louder 'til it couldn't possibly get any louder. Only it did.

It was then we heard the crash. Then silence. Only a dog barking in the distance.

10   'Eric, something's got shot down,' said Albert.

'Shall we go and look?'

'He might be trapped … He might be …'

It was unsayable. But we went.

It looked as big as a house.

15   'Spitfire.'

'Hurricane, you idiot. Can't you tell a Spitfire from a Hurricane yet?'

'It's not badly damaged. Just a bit bent.'

I shook my head. 'It'll never fly again. It looks … broke.'

The tail was up in the air; the engine dug right into the ground, and
20   the propeller bent into horseshoe shapes.

'Where's the pilot?'

'He might have baled out,' suggested Albert, hopefully.

'What? At that height? His parachute would never have opened. Reckon he's trapped inside. We'd better have a look.'

25 'Eric, keep well back,' said Albert. 'There's a terrible smell of petrol. I saw petrol take fire once …'

I was so scared my legs wouldn't stop shaking. But it was me that went in front. The cockpit canopy was closed. Inside, from a distance, there was no sign of any pilot.

30 'Baled out. Told ya,' said Albert.

'With the canopy closed?'

'The crash could've closed it, stupid.'

'I'm going to have a look.'

I edged up on the wing, frightened that my steel toe and heel caps would
35 strike a spark from something. He was inside. Bent up double, with only the back of his helmet showing. And there was a great tear in the side of the helmet, with leather and stuffing … and blood showing through.

'He's a dead 'un,' said Albert, six inches behind my ear. I hadn't even heard him come – he was wearing gym-shoes. 'Look at that blood.'

40 I felt sick. The only dead thing I'd ever seen was a cat.

'Let's go an' fetch the police,' said Albert. 'They deal with dead 'uns.'

I was edging carefully back down the wing, when a flicker of movement in the corner of my eye made me jump.

The dead 'un was sitting up.

45 The dead 'un was looking at me with two bright blue eyes.

The dead 'un grinned at me. Made a little 'hello' gesture with his gloved hand. His hand went up, and he undid a catch and pushed the canopy back, where it locked open.

'Hi, kids.' He sounded American, or at least Canadian.

50 'Boy, have I got a headache! Haven't got a fag, have you?'

Adapted from *The Ruined City of Kor* by Robert Westall

❓ What's it all about?

1   Imagine that the two boys were interviewed by a local newspaper. How would they answer these questions about finding the aircraft?

   a   When did you realise that a plane was crashing? (lines 1–9)

   It was when we heard ... After this we heard ... Finally there was the sound of ...

   b   What were you thinking when you went up to the plane? (lines 27–33)

   Walking up to the plane I was thinking about ... I was so scared that ...

   c   Where did the pilot come from? (lines 46–50)

   We knew he came from ... because ...

   d   Why did you think the pilot was still inside? (lines 28–32)

   We knew he was inside when we saw ...

   e   Who had the idea to check the cockpit? (lines 21–26)

   That was ... He wanted to look because ...

Looking at the detail

2   First read the key points on page 73. Then answer the following questions about the ways that tension is built up.

Lines 1–9: The description of SOUNDS makes the reader expect something

   a   What did the boys hear first? What did they sound like?

   b   What did the boys hear next? What happened to the noise?

   c   What could be heard after the sound of the crash?

Lines 12–41: The boys are AFRAID, which develops the tension

   d   The boys start to argue because they are afraid. What do they disagree about?

   e   Why does a smell frighten Albert?

   f   Why does Albert say that Eric is stupid?

   g   Why is Eric frightened by his steel toe-caps?

Lines 42–50: The tension builds to a SURPRISE ENDING

   h   How does the pilot look when Eric looks in the cockpit?

   i   What do the boys call the pilot? How many times do they say it?

   j   What surprising thing then happens?

The big question

3   **How does the writer build up tension in this passage?**

Use your answers to the questions above to help you. In your answer you should write about:

- how the descriptions of sound make the reader expect something to happen

  The boys hear a number of sounds, starting with … This builds tension because …

- how the tension builds up as the boys become more frightened

  We can tell the boys are frightened because … They begin to …

- the surprise ending

  At first we think that … We think this because … Then …

Remember to use quotations in your answer. Turn to pages 56–57 for more help with using quotations.

Key points

- Tension is what you feel when you are waiting for something important to happen.
- Writers build up tension to make you want to read on to find out what happens next.
- The writer of this passage uses sounds, fear and a surprise ending to build up the tension.

Read the newspaper article below. The RSPCA were asked to rescue a goldfish which was being cruelly treated by some teenagers.

You are going to answer the question:

How does the newspaper story grab and keep the reader's attention?

GOLDFISH RESCUED FROM TREE

Pet floats off as yobs tie it to six helium balloons

AN RSPCA officer rushed to the rescue on Saturday after astonished passers-by reported a goldfish stuck 15 feet up a TREE.

Kevin Cunningham, 39, was called in after a gang of 5 teeny yobs tied the fairground prize and its plastic bag of water to six helium-filled balloons.

Ordeal

They watched as the 'flying fish' took off and drifted into trees. Then they pelted it with bricks, sticks and stones when it got
10 lodged in the branches.

They finally fled after a furious passer-by told them he was reporting them to the RSPCA.

Kevin, a chief inspector with the RSPCA,
15 used a pole to unhook the bag from the tree and lower the fish to the ground as it gasped for life.

He said: 'The fish was not moving and very close to death. It had been through a
20 terrible ordeal.

'When I received the call saying, "There's a fish up a tree," I thought it was some sort of joke. But I soon realised the caller was serious.

25 'Apparently the kids had told him the RSPCA wouldn't bother to come out if it was "only" a fish. But my response is that we'd go out to any living creature that was suffering.

'These children did not have any care for
30 the quality of life of that fish. I'm just pleased I was able to save it. There wasn't much water left in the bag and it wasn't far from suffocating.

'It's my most bizarre rescue in nine years'
35 *service. You see some weird sights but a fish up a tree is a first.'*

The pet – nicknamed **Biggles** by RSPCA staff – is now recovering at the home of a local fish enthusiast in New Bolsover, Derbyshire.
40 The balloon attack is believed to have happened after the children won the fish at a fairground stall.

Kevin said: 'This fish has been terribly abused. The RSPCA has been **campaigning**
45 for fairs to stop giving them out as prizes – they usually get flushed down the loo.

'You should not give animals away. People say it's only a goldfish, but it's a life like any other.'

The Sun

---

bizarre: *strange*
Biggles: *a character in a book who flew aeroplanes*
campaigning: *working to change people's opinions and behaviour*

What's it all about?

1 Work in pairs. One of you is the RSPCA officer. The other is the journalist interviewing him. Improvise their conversation. Use the notes below to help you, and make your own.

Journalist	RSPCA officer
What is the strangest call …?	When I had to rescue …
What had happened …?	The fish had … It was …
Who did …?	A group … they had won …
Why did …?	The teenagers thought it was only …
When did …?	A passer-by …
What did you think when …?	At first … but then …
Where is …?	'Biggles' is now …
How do the RSPCA feel about …?	Even a fish is … Animals should not be …

 Looking at the detail

Read lines 1–13.

2 Why does the newspaper heading grab readers' attention?

3 Pick out three details which show how cruel the teenagers were.

Read lines 14–36.

4 Pick out two details which make you feel sorry for the fish.

5 Copy out and complete the time line to show how Kevin's thoughts and feelings about the fish changed.

At first … ➜ But I soon … ➜ I'm just pleased … ➜ It's my most …

Read lines 37–49.

6 This part of the article contains a lot of facts and opinions. Find the facts and opinions Kevin uses to argue that fish should not be given away as fairground prizes. Copy out and complete the chart below.

Facts	Opinions
… the children won the fish …	These children did not have any care for the quality of life …
There wasn't much …	You should not give …
The RSPCA have been …	People say it's … but …

The big question

7 **How does the newspaper story grab and keep the reader's attention?**

- The story grabs your attention because the headlines make ...

- The writer shows how cruel the teenagers are ...

- Readers are made to feel sorry for the fish because ...

- Kevin Cunningham's part in the story makes it ... At first ...

- It makes you think about whether fairgrounds ...

Key points

A newspaper article has to grab the reader's attention.

It should tell you the answers to these questions:

Who was involved?

    What happened?

       When?

          Where?

          Why?

Look back at page 18 for more help on reading newspaper articles.

B5 US flies in Hamburgers

Read the poem on the opposite page. Roger McGough saw the newspaper headline: *US flies in Hamburgers*. The story was actually about flying in hamburgers to American troops. Roger McGough had different ideas and wrote this poem.

You are going to answer the question:

How does Roger McGough turn a newspaper headline into a poem that is both humorous and horrible?

 ## What's it all about?

1 Read the whole poem through again. Write a sentence to say what the poem is about.

2 Read lines 11–20. Make a list of all the creatures that the poet says are being put into burgers.

 ## Remember

A sound effect you often find in poetry is **alliteration**. This is where words begin with the same letter:

Baltimore bedbugs

Can you spot two more examples of alliteration in Roger McGough's poem?

Look back at page 50 to find out more about sound effects in poetry.

US flies in Hamburgers

If you go down the High Street today
You'll be sure of a big surprise,
When you order your favourite burger
With a milkshake and regular fries.

5 For the secret is out
I tell you no lies
They've stopped using beef
In favour of FLIES

FLIES, FLIES, big juicy FLIES,
10 FLIES as American as apple pies

Horseflies, from Texas, as big as your thumb
Are sautéd with onions and served in a bun.

Free-range bluebottles, carefully rinsed
Are smothered in garlic and painlessly minced.

15 Black-eyed bees with stings intact
Add a zesty zing, and that's a fact.

Colorado beetles, ants from Kentucky,
Rhode Island roaches, and if you're unlucky

Baltimore bedbugs (and even horrider)
20 Leeches as squashy as peaches from Florida.

FLIES, FLIES, big juicy FLIES
FLIES as American as mom's apple pies.

It's lovely down in MacDingle's today
But if you don't fancy flies
25 Better I'd say to keep well away
Stay home and eat Birds' Eyes.

by Roger McGough

sautéd: *fried*
zesty zing: *pleasant but sharp taste*

Looking at the detail

3 Read line 13. Pick out the words that make these new burgers sound healthy.

4 Read lines 9–16. Choose the words and phrases that make the burgers sound tasty.

5 The children's song *The Teddy Bears' Picnic* begins with almost the same words as Roger McGough's poem. What is the effect of this? Write out each of these comments. Choose the words in bold that you agree with.

> *You expect something that's suitable for young children and you get **what you expect / a shock / a surprise.***

> *It makes sure that the tone is **silly / absurd / comic / ridiculous** from the beginning.*

6 Look at the boxes below. Write out the sentence that you think is best.

makes it sound like a chant.

The regular rhythm

makes the poem quiet and ordinary.

gives a sense of things steadily building up.

7 Look at the Key Points box on page 81. Copy and complete these sentences.

The four-line stanzas in the poem rhyme at the end of the _____ and the _____ lines. In the last stanza lines _____ and _____ also rhyme. The rest of the poem is written in _____ couplets.

8 Read the statements below. Copy out the ones you agree with. Write a sentence of your own about the rhymes in the poem.

   a   The rhymes add to the sense of fun.

   b   The rhymes keep you reading.

   c   The rhymes make it sound like a song.

9 Which part of the poem is the most horrible? Explain why you chose it.

10 Which part of the poem is the most humorous? Explain why you chose it.

11 **How does Roger McGough turn a newspaper headline into a poem that is both humorous and horrible?**

Use your answers to the questions on pages 78 and 80 and this framework to help you.

The first thing the poet changes is the story behind the ... The poem is not about feeding troops but instead the poem says that ... It is not just any old ... that are being used. Roger McGough describes a whole range of creatures: ... The poem makes these new burgers sound quite tasty as it describes how ... The poet even manages to make them seem healthy by saying ...

Roger McGough begins his poem by using almost the same words as ... The effect of this is to ...

The regular rhythm ... The poem begins and ends with ... line stanzas which rhyme at the end of the ... The last stanza also rhymes ... The rest of the poem is written in ... couplets. The rhymes in the poem ... Roger McGough gets the sense of horror across best in the part ... I think the humour works best when ...

 ## Key points

- A verse in a poem is called a **stanza**.
- A two-line stanza is called a **couplet**. When the two lines rhyme, it is called a *rhyming couplet*.

Look back at pages 48–55 to find out more about reading poetry.

B6 Eyesight agony

Read the advertisement on the opposite page. It tells readers how they can help to stop people suffering from eye diseases.

You are going to answer the question:

How does the advertisement persuade you to give money to Sight Savers?

? What's it all about?

1 Read these summaries of the advertisement. Put them in order, starting with the one you think is best.

a The advertisement gives you advice about stopping trachoma and asks you to buy some ointment.

b A charity is asking for money to help it cure people with trachoma.

c The advertisement tells you that people pull out eyelashes if they get trachoma.

2 Read the advertisement again. Complete these statements about what trachoma can do to people.

a Trachoma makes eyelashes … (lines 6–7).

b The eyelashes scrape … which means … (lines 7–10).

c People use tweezers to … because … (lines 9–14).

d The eyelashes grow … which causes … (lines 14–16).

Remember

Advertising is about getting a message across to the reader.

Advertisements try to persuade you to do something. They often want you to spend money.

When you read advertisements look out for

- **P**roduct
- **A**udience

- **M**essage
- **A**ppeal

For more help, look back at page 24–29.

IT'S WHAT ALL THE GIRLS ARE WEARING THESE DAYS

In many parts of Africa and Asia, young women are wearing tweezers around their neck. This has nothing to do with fashion. They have trachoma, a horrific
5 infection that scars their eyelids. This causes their eyelashes to turn inwards. Every time they blink the eyelashes scrape against their eyes. The result is agony, and then they
10 go blind.

You'd pull out your eyelashes, too

In desperation many people pull out their eyelashes with tweezers. Who wouldn't? But the eyelashes
15 grow back, stronger than before, causing even greater damage.

AND YOU CAN SEE WHY

The cost of stopping this agony? Just £1.20

Trachoma is easy to stop with just a small tube of ointment, which only costs £1.20. That means a gift of £12 from you would be enough to treat TEN people. You could stop their agony and help to save their sight.

Please give the gift of sight

Sight Savers is a charity that helps to cure blindness. But to treat people with trachoma and other eye diseases we need help. We need people who will give a little of their money to save the sight of
30 others.

Please send us a gift now and help save more people from the terrible pain of blindness and trachoma.

Here is my gift of:

£12 ☐ £25 ☐ £50 ☐ £125 ☐ £250 ☐

35 **Other £** _____

Please make your cheque payable to Sight Savers International, or if you wish to pay by MasterCard, Visa, Switch, Amex or CAF Charity Card, enter your card number in the boxes below.

☐☐☐☐☐☐☐☐☐☐☐☐☐☐☐☐☐☐

40 Card Expiry Date ____/____ Issue No. (Switch) _____
Mr/Mrs/Miss/Ms ____ Initials _____ Surname _____
Address _____
_____ Postcode _____
45 Signature _____

To make your credit card gift work faster, please call our hotline on:

07000 14 20 20

Please detach this form and return it, with your gift, to:
50 **Sight Savers International, Room No. IN68, FREEPOST, Haywards Heath, West Sussex RH16 4BR**

ROYAL COMMONWEALTH SOCIETY FOR THE BLIND
Registered Charity Number: 207544

The layout of an advertisement helps to persuade you. How does the layout of this advertisement grab and keep your attention? Answer the questions below.

3 Find two ways that the main headline and the caption under the photo look different from the rest of the text.

4 Write down the three subheadings in this advertisement.

5 Describe what each photo in the Sight Savers advertisement shows you. How does it make you want to read the text?

 Remember

Headings

> **H**eadlines stand out from the rest of the text to catch your eye.

> Subheadings make important points stand out. They make you want to read the text. They are usually bolder than the other text.

Illustrations

> **I**llustrations (pictures) make you want to find out more.

Prose

For more help turn back to page 16.

6 Read the following statements about trachoma. They are all based on the prose part of the advertisement. Decide whether each one is a fact or an opinion. How does each one make you feel sorry for these young women?

a In many parts of Africa and Asia, young women are wearing tweezers around their neck.

b Trachoma causes eyelashes to turn inwards.

c If you had trachoma, you'd pull your eyelashes out too.

d You could stop their agony and help to save their sight.

Statement **a** is a … . It makes you feel sorry for these young women because …

7 The advertisement also makes readers feel they can help. Choose three statements below that make you feel you can help. Explain how each one persuades people to give.

a The cost of preventing this agony? Just £1.20.

b That means a gift of £12 from you would be enough to treat TEN people.

c The result is agony, then blindness.

d We need people who will give a little of their money to save the sight of others.

e They have trachoma, a horrific infection that scars their eyelids.

? ## The big question

8 **How does the advertisement persuade you to give money to Sight Savers?**

Use your answers to the questions above to help you. In your answer you should write about:

- **how the advertisement is written and set out on the page:**
  The important points … They also use … because …

- **how readers are made to feel sorry for people with trachoma:**
  Trachoma is described as … This makes you feel …

- **how readers are made to feel they can help:**
  Curing trachoma is … you need … which costs …

B7 Explosion!

Read the following play extract. It is set in the First World War, in a factory that makes bombs and bullets. Working in the factory is very dangerous.

You are going to answer the questions:

- How does the writer show you that Winnie is upset?

- Who does Winnie blame for the explosion?

Explosion!

Maggie (*to audience*) I was just thinking it was too good to last when half the shell-filling workshop blew up. All the windows smashed. I was still picking glass out of me clothes when Winnie Fawcett came in.

5 *Winnie enters. Her eyes are full of anger and tears. The others stop clearing up and stare at her.*

Maggie The skin was burnt off one side of her face, and there was blood running down her arm …

Winnie That's right! Have a good look! … Will you do something now,
10 eh? Will you men do something now? They've just carried three lasses dead out of my workshop! I know we're only women like, but are you going to let the bosses get away with this? 'Cos they won't listen to us, you know. They're making bloody millions out of this war, and everybody knows it! So,
15 you men, you tell the bosses to spend some of their bloody money, and get some proper machines for us! And stop working us seventy and eighty hours a week!
Or you'll come out on strike for us!
(*She looks at them all.*)
20 Well, you men?

Frank Clayton? Are you going to tell them this time, or are you going to wait till the whole bloody lot goes up?! *Frank goes to Winnie and puts his arm round her.*

	Frank	Come on, lass. I know you're upset, but we're not to blame for this. It's the bosses, and you know it.
25		
	Jack	Aye, it's not our fault, missis. So don't come in here, crying at us.
	Frank	(*holding her*) She's upset, Jack, that's all.
	Maggie	'Course she's upset! She's just been blown up! She's every right to be flaming upset!
30	**Jack**	Don't you start, bonny lass.
	Frank	Just calm down, alright?
	Maggie	I don't want to calm down! I want something done!
	Frank	Alright! (*to Winnie*) I'll talk to the lads, then I'll talk to Barrington. You know me, Winnie. I'll do me best for you.
35	**Winnie**	Aye, Frank, I know. I'm sorry.

Adapted from *Filling the Shells* by Paul Swift

1 Match each character to a description.

Frank	Does not like people who moan.
Winnie	Stands up for friends and talks to audience.
Maggie	Promises to try to help.
Jack	Very upset and injured.

2 Write down which parts of the stage directions show you that:

   a Maggie is telling the audience what happened.

   b Winnie is upset and full of rage.

   c Everyone is shocked at the sight of Winnie.

   d Frank moves across to one person in particular.

   e Frank takes Winnie's side against Jack.

 Key points

1 • In a fiction book the story is often told from somebody's point of view. They can tell you about things that have happened in different times and places. You can also read about what they are thinking.

   • In a play you can only see what is happening on the stage now. Sometimes the writer makes a character tell the audience about things that you have not seen happen on stage. Maggie does this at the beginning of this extract. They may also tell you how they feel about something.

2 In a play script you have to work out what characters are like from:

   • what they say (the *dialogue*)

   • how they treat others

   • what other characters say about them

   • how other characters treat them

   • stage directions that show how they talk and act.

3 The way drama is set out on the page can make it seem long. Do not let this put you off!

Looking at the detail

3 Write down what Winnie looked like when she came into the workshop. (Look at lines 5–8.)

4 Winnie blames her bosses for the explosion. She also is upset because the male workers will not stand up for the women. Read lines 9–22. Then complete her thought bubbles.

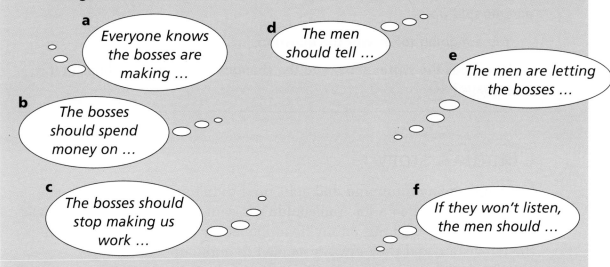

a Everyone knows the bosses are making …

b The bosses should spend money on …

c The bosses should stop making us work …

d The men should tell …

e The men are letting the bosses …

f If they won't listen, the men should …

 ## The big question 1

5 **How does the writer show you that Winnie is upset?**

In your answer you should talk about:

- how Winnie looks when she enters the workshop:

  Her face is … her eyes are … blood is coming from …

- the stage directions:

  They show that Winnie … The directions show others are …

- the things Winnie says:

  She tells the men … After this she says … Finally she …

 ## The big question 2

6 **Who does Winnie blame for the explosion?**

In your answer you should talk about:

- what Winnie thinks of the bosses and the men she works with:

  Winnie believes that … because … The … are also at fault because …

B8 Gone!

> Read the following passage. Claudia is remembering the time when her parents split up.
>
> You are going to answer the question:
>
> How does the writer show you the changes in Claudia's feelings in this passage?

Claudia's story

Not long ago my mum and dad split up. I didn't see it coming. I knew that they quarrelled a lot. You couldn't miss it. But I didn't think it was anything special. I'd put on my headphones, or turn up the sound on the television, and they always seemed to make up again pretty
5 quickly. One day my mum would be moaning about my dad:

'I'm fed up with the way he spends all his time running that café. We hardly ever see him, and when we do, he's too tired to be pleasant.'

But the next day, if I said anything, she'd take a fit.

'Don't talk about Daddy like that, please!'

10 And then, one day, he was gone. I came home from school, and everything in the house was moved around. My bedroom radio was in the kitchen. My jackets and shoes were spread out more neatly in the downstairs cupboard because all his coats and boots had disappeared. The frog mug I gave him for his birthday wasn't on its hook. And some
15 of the photos round the house were gone – just ones of me and him.

'What's going on?'

'Nothing,' Mum said. 'It's just that your father and I aren't getting on very well at the moment, so he's gone to Granny's house while we calm down.'

20 She tried to sound cheerful about it. But I knew it was worse than she was letting on. (Usually, he calms down working at the café, and she calms down on the phone to her sister. No one had ever gone to calm down at Granny's before. And no one had ever taken a radio and wellies and photos.)

25   He came back quite a lot at first. Not to stay. Just for tea (and more
arguments). I'm not completely stupid. Sometimes I listened behind
doors, and sometimes I switched my headphones up so loudly that they
leaked, but didn't put them in my ears properly, so Mum and Dad didn't
realise I was **eavesdropping** as I walked past them and up the stairs
30 to my bedroom. And sometimes I asked the two of them:

'What's going on?'

'Nothing,' they kept saying. 'Don't worry. It will all be sorted out.'

Then, suddenly, everything changed. There was a flood of phone calls
late one night, and Mum was in a rage, and even Granny (who'd been
35 very busy 'not taking sides') had a huge row with Dad. And that was
the first time I heard the name 'Stella'. Mum spat it down the phone to
her sister so hard that I had to write it on a sheet of paper in curly felt-
pen letters and stare at it, before it turned back from a swear word to a
name again.

40   And, after that, my dad hardly dared come near the house.

Step By Wicked Step by Anne Fine

eavesdropping: listening secretly

1 Claudia's best friend asks her some questions. Write down the answers that Claudia would give.

    a What did you do when your parents used to quarrel? (lines 1–4)

        Usually I'd put on … or …

    b What happened on the day your dad left? (lines 10–20)

        Things had been moved, such as … Other things were gone, like …

    c Did your mum say anything when he left? (lines 16–24)

        She said that … and that he'd gone to …

    d Did he come back to visit? What was it like? (lines 25–32)

        At first … but they would still … I would pretend … but really I was …

    e Why doesn't he visit any more? (lines 33–40)

        Late one night … I heard the name … Mum was …

 Remember

Show why your ideas are right by using quotations from the text. Make sure you copy the word or phrase exactly and put it inside quotation marks. For example:

    'He came back quite a lot at first.'

For extra help with using quotations, look back at pages 56–57.

 Key points

1 A writer sometimes tells you exactly how characters are feeling. At other times you have to work out how they are feeling from what the writer makes them *think*, *say* and *do*.

2 This story is written in the **first person**. Claudia is telling the story herself. This gives you a good picture from her point of view. But remember that Claudia cannot see and understand everything.

Looking at the detail

2 Copy out and complete the table below. First read each clue, then find the right quotation using the line numbers to help you. Lastly, write down what the quotation and the clue tell you about Claudia's feelings.

	Line numbers	These details ... (*find a quotation*)	... give you a clue ...	... which suggests ...
What Claudia says	16–19	'What's going on?'	Claudia does not know where her dad is.	Claudia is very confused.
	31		Claudia is still worried about the arguments.	Claudia is not sure if she is being told the truth.
What Claudia thinks	1–5		Claudia heard the quarrelling but took no notice.	Claudia didn't think that ...
	20–21	'I knew it was worse than she was letting on.'	Claudia listens to what Mum says about Dad leaving.	
What Claudia does	26–30		Claudia pretends to be doing something else.	
	36–39		Claudia stares at the name she has scribbled on paper.	

The big question

3 **How does the writer show you the changes in Claudia's feelings in this passage?**

Use your answer to question **1** and your chart to help you. In your answer you should write about:

- what Claudia thinks and feels at first
- Claudia's thoughts and feelings as things develop
- Claudia's reaction to the shock discovery at the end.

Remember to use quotations to support what you say.

B9 Fox Farm

Read the following poem. It is about a farmer who keeps foxes to sell for their fur.

You are going to answer the question:

How does the writer make you feel sorry for the fox?

Fox Farm

The silver fox
with glossy fur,
penned in its man-made den,
paces the prison
5 yard of its cage
again, again, again.

The farmer sneers:
'Why should I care?
I'm not breaking the law.'
10 The restless fox
prowls without pause
a wire-mesh **tundra** floor.

The fashion-hounds
dripping with scent,
15 admire and stroke his **pelt**.
The farmer shrugs,
pleads innocence,
stuffs banknotes in his belt.

by John Foster

tundra: *a place where there are few plants and the soil is always frozen*
pelt: *the skin of an animal with the fur still on*
pleads: *claims. This word is usually used in a court room*

What's it all about?

1 Choose the best summary of the poem. Give reasons for your choice.

   a A farmer has caught a fox and is keeping it in a cage as a pet.

   b A farmer breeds foxes and sells them for their fur.

   c People pay a farmer to come and look at his caged animals.

2 Match each picture to the right stanza of the poem.

A    **B**    **C**

Looking at the detail

3 How do the words the poet has chosen make you feel sorry for the fox?

Words or phrases that make you dislike how the fox is treated 	**a** Line 3 **b** Line 4 **c** Line 5 **d** Line 10 **e** Line 11 **f** Line 12	*penned in*
Words or phrases that make you dislike the farmer 	**g** Line 7 **h** Line 8 **i** Line 16 **j** Line 18	*sneers*
Words or phrases that make you dislike the buyers 	**k** Line 13 **l** Line 14 **m** Line 15	*fashion hounds*
Words that make you like the fox 	**n** Line 1 **o** Line 2	*silver*

4 Read the poem aloud so you can hear the rhyme and repetition. Remember that you only need to pause if there is a full-stop or a comma on the end of a line. Look back at page 48 to find out more about reading a poem aloud. Before you start, find:

   a two words that rhyme at the end of the line in each stanza

   b three words that are repeated. How do they make you feel sorry for the fox?

5 Which is the best description of the sound of the poem?

   a A fast, regular beat with no rhymes, making it sound exciting.

   b A slow, regular beat with a regular rhyme, making it sound sad.

   c No rhymes and a beat that is different in every stanza, making it sound like the farmer's conversation.

6 Look at the poem's word pictures. Why do you think the writer has chosen these images? Copy and complete the table below.

Line number	Image	What is being compared or described	Why the image has been chosen
		The floor of the cage is compared with tundra.	The tundra is cold and bare and an awful place to be.
		The people buying the fox fur are called 'hounds' like the dogs used in a fox-hunt.	These people and real hounds both kill the fox.
		The buyers wear so much perfume that it is described as 'dripping'.	Real hounds find and follow a fox by following its natural scent.

 Remember

Words, sound effects and 'pictures' all work together to create the meaning.
Turn to pages 48–55 for help with reading poetry.

 Key points

People who write poems choose words very carefully for the effect they have. For example:

   stuffs *banknotes in his belt*

The words *puts*, *places*, *locates* or *sites* could be used instead of *stuffs*. Each word has a different effect on the reader. The word *stuffs* makes the farmer sound greedy. This is what the writer wants you to think.

? The big question

7 **How does the writer make you feel sorry for the fox?**

In your answer you should talk about:

- **The words and phrases that the writer uses. Use your answers to question 3 to help you:**

  Words such as … and … describe how the fox is treated. This makes you think … When the poem says that the farmer … you think that … When the farmer says: …

- **The sound effects in the poem. Look back at your answers to questions 4 and 5.**

  The writer repeats the word … which makes you feel … The beat of the poem is … which makes the poem sound …

- **The word pictures the writer creates. Use the table you completed in question 6.**

  When the writer compares the floor of the cage with … it makes you feel … When he calls the buyers …, it makes you remember that wild foxes are often … Both kinds of … want to … The writer uses the words … in line 14 to …

B10 She's electric!

Read the following article which appeared in a teenage magazine. It is about a girl called Katrine who suffers from an unusual illness.

You are going to answer the question:

How does the writer make the information about Sliders interesting for teenage readers?

SHE'S ELECTRIC!

When 16-year-old Katrine Kirkman – 'Sparky' to her friends – gets angry, excited or stressed out, weird things begin to happen …

My friends and family have called me 'Sparky' ever since I can remember because when I'm around, light bulbs explode, TVs
5 fuse, ovens overheat and computers crash – but no one knows why. For years, Mum and Dad just thought it was a coincidence that these things
10 happened when I was around, and they joked about it. But eventually they got **suspicious** and took me to a doctor.

The doctor sent me to a
15 **specialist** who **diagnosed** me as having a very rare **condition** known as Sliders, which is short for Street Light Interference Data

Exchange. He told me that people
20 who suffer from Sliders affect electrical equipment – often street lights, which is how it got its name – because they have an unusually high build-up of static
25 electricity in their bodies. When this electrical charge gets to a certain level (something amazing, like 500 000 volts) it **discharges** from the body and

'I blew all the lights on the big wheel'

suspicious: *feeling that something is wrong*
specialist: *a doctor who knows a lot about one kind of disease*
diagnosed: *found out what was wrong*
condition: *a medical problem*
discharges: *goes out of suddenly*

can cause electrical equipment to short circuit!

By the time I was 14 it had got to the point where Mum and Dad had given up buying new gadgets for the house and hired them all instead. They just couldn't afford to keep replacing the equipment I somehow destroyed. Over the years they reckon I have broken six TVs, three fridges, eight radios, two CD players, two blenders, an oven, a microwave, a computer, seven watches, hundreds of light bulbs and my grandma's hearing aid; and cost them about £3000 – oops!

Sometimes my strange powers get me into really embarrassing situations. A couple of years ago I went to the fairground with my boyfriend and, although I really hated heights, he persuaded me to go on the Big Wheel. I had my eyes tightly closed but when we got to the top I opened them and was so frightened I blew the Big Wheel's motor. All the lights went out and we were stuck, dangling a hundred feet in the air for over an hour while people below had to handwinch the wheel around to let everyone off. Of course, no one knew it was me who blew the motor, but I couldn't help but feel slightly guilty as I clambered out of the chair and past the smoking engine.

I suppose my mates have got used to me now. At first, some thought it was a bit spooky and weird, but no one gives me a hard time about it – I suppose because it doesn't happen all the time. I can sometimes go for a few months without anything happening at all.

I'm apparently one of only a very small handful of sufferers in the world, so it's very, very rare. The last figure I heard was that there are 138 known cases of Sliders in the whole world. Of that figure, 65 per cent of sufferers are under the age of 25 and 67 per cent are girls.

No one knows why certain people suffer from this condition while others don't, because so little research has been done. But some people think that it's due to sufferers living near power lines, and others say that it's some sort of psychic energy.

I don't think doctors will ever find a cure for Sliders, but I don't care – it hasn't done me any harm. And besides, my new boyfriend loves it. He says my kisses are electric! ∎

Mizz

What's it all about?

1 You have been asked to give a short talk about what Sliders is to a Primary school class. Make brief notes under these four headings.

> **What is Sliders?**
> **What happens to people who suffer from it?**
> **How common is it?**
> **Is there any cure?**

Looking at the detail

2 Read lines 1–13 and 32–45 where Katrine tells the reader how the disease has affected her.

  a Why do you think the writer chose Katrine's story for teenage readers?

  b What sorts of problems does Katrine's illness cause?

3 Read lines 46–66. Katrine tells us about one incident. Why might teenage readers find it particularly interesting?

4 Read lines 1–31 and 76–92.

  a Write down four facts you are given about Sliders.

  b Why might the writer have decided to give the reader information about Sliders in chunks rather than all together in one go?

  c Copy out and complete the chart below. It shows people's opinions about Katrine's illness. Why do you think the writer included these?

People	Opinion
parents	at first they thought it was just coincidence ...
friends	
boyfriend	
Katrine	

5 Find two words or phrases in the first paragraph which make Katrine's illness sound mysterious.

6 Why might the last paragraph make Sliders sound appealing to teenage readers?

7 Read what four people said about the article. Which opinion do you agree with most? Find three quotations to support your choice.

A
> It's a very serious article written in a formal tone.

B
> It's quite chatty and light-hearted but contains practical advice and guidance.

C
> It's informal and makes Sliders sound serious but mysterious and exciting too.

D
> It's humorous and full of stories which make you wonder if Sliders really exists.

 ## The big question

8 **How does the writer make the information about Sliders interesting for teenage readers?**

In your answer you should include:

- how the writer uses Katrine's experience of having Sliders to give information about the condition
- how facts and opinions are used
- how the article is organised
- how the disease and its effects are described.

 ## Key points

1 Information in an article is always broken down to make it more readable. In this article, each paragraph gives you different information about Sliders.

2 When you answer a big question like the one in this unit:

  a use the suggestions to help you organise your answer

  b aim to write at least one paragraph about each suggestion

  c go through the text making notes and picking out quotations to use when you write about each suggestion.

B11 Save the Children Week

Read the leaflet on pages 103 and 104. Save the Children is a charity which works all over the world helping young people. This is a leaflet they produced to tell people about their work.

You are going to answer two questions:

- What do you learn about how Save the Children spends your money in Vietnam?

- How does this leaflet try to persuade you that your money will be well spent?

 ## What's it all about?

Look at the information on Vietnam on page 104.

1 Copy and complete this sentence.

People in Thanh Hoa often only have the money to plant rice, so if the rice harvest fails they ...

2 How much did Doe borrow?

3 What did she do once she was given the money?

4 Why is she glad to pay back what she borrowed?

 ## Key points

- Leaflets give you information. People often hope you will respond by buying something, giving something or by getting involved. Sometimes people simply hope that the information will change your view about a subject. Leaflets usually carry more information than an advertisement.

- Leaflets have a *target audience*. These are the people that the publishers of the leaflet hope will use it. The target audience for a leaflet on bus times are the people who might use those buses.

- Leaflets also invite people to respond. People respond by
  - doing something, *such as using the buses described in a leaflet*
  - giving money, *to a charity like Save the Children*
  - spending money *on the things that a leaflet is advertising*
  - changing their ideas, *such as learning that an illness can be cured.*

A luxury chocolate **gateau** costs £4.99

UK

VIETNAM

Photo: Jenny Matthews

£4 A £4 loan to a mother in Vietnam will help her raise crops and **livestock**

gateau: *fancy cake*
livestock: *farm animals*

lending

In the poor Thanh Hoa district of Vietnam, many people own nothing except their land. What little money they have is spent on planting rice. They have to depend entirely on their rice harvest and it often fails.

5 In an area like this, a Save the Children lending scheme can do much to improve people's **circumstances**, changing the lives of families like Doe's.

A while ago, Doe borrowed about £4 from her local scheme. She used the money to buy a few chicks. Now
10 she has over 30 chickens. She sold eggs and some of the birds to buy a piglet. Once it was fattened, she sold the pig to buy two more piglets and used one to pay back her loan.

Doe is happy to repay the money, because she knows that it means another family in turn can have a loan to help
15 them provide the food they need.

As she says: 'Before I got the loan I didn't know what to do.' But today, thanks to the lending scheme, her children are fed and she is much more confident about their future.

Save the Children WEEK
27 APRIL – 3 MAY

Many children's parents can't afford to buy the food they need

circumstances: *situation (especially in terms of money)*

5 Look at the first page of the leaflet on page 103. It tells you about what money can buy. Put these responses in order, so that the most important goes first.

A
> It shows you how expensive things are in Britain.

B
> It shows how cheap things can be in Vietnam.

C
> It shows what a big difference you could make by giving up a small luxury.

D
> It shows what good value you can get if you give money to this charity.

6 The picture of Vietnam shows a girl in the field. Why? Choose the best answer.

a
> A field of crops is boring.

b
> The charity concentrates on children.

c
> It shows that work is needed.

d
> A child looking out at you may encourage people to give.

7 Read lines 13–15 on page 104. Doe has repaid the loan. Why might this make people more willing to give to the charity?

8 Read lines 16–18 on page 104. How has the loan changed Doe's life?

? The big question

9 a **What do you learn about how Save the Children spends your money in Vietnam?** Write about:
  - the situation in Thanh Hoa
  - what Doe did
  - how the loan is repaid
  - what happens to the money that is repaid.

  b **How does this leaflet try to persuade you that your money will be well spent?** Comment on:
  - what the first page of the leaflet says about money
  - how the pictures are used
  - the loan as value for money
  - the effect on people's lives.

B12 · I don't like cricket!

> Read the following passage. Johnny leads a gang of bullies. They have tied
> Timothy to the cricket stumps in the cricket nets. Johnny has taken
> Timothy's glasses and trumpet. He is wearing Timothy's glasses. There is
> about to be a terrible thunderstorm.
>
> You are going to answer this question:
>
> How does the writer build up to the surprise ending?

Flash!

'Where's my trumpet?' Timothy asked.

'Safe as houses,' said Johnny, putting the brass instrument in his
right hand. A streak of lightning lit up the sky over the common. The
rain pricked Timothy's face like pins.

5   'Now here's what we're going to do. We're going to bowl at you,
Timothy,' Johnny explained.

'But I need a bat and pads and gloves …' Timothy said.

'Why?' said Johnny.

'Or the balls will hit me!' quaked Timothy.

10   'I do hope so!' said Johnny. 'That's why I've gone to the trouble of
tying you up.'

The thunder crashed above their heads like cannons of war and
drove the rain down like bullets from a machine gun.

'Have fun, my son. Duck and weave,' laughed Johnny. He walked
15   back up to the net at the bowling end. Timothy slipped on the muddy
ground as he tried to push his way out through the netting.

'Oh, by the way,' called Johnny, 'I thought I'd play you a little tune on
the trumpet while my friends are bowling. Any requests?'

'Don't do this!' wailed Timothy. 'Please!'

20   'Don't know that one,' snickered Johnny, much to his gang's
amusement. 'I thought I'd do "I Don't Like Cricket" if it's all the same
to you!'

And with that Johnny gave a signal to his bowlers to start bowling whilst he put the trumpet to his lips to start trumpeting.

25　There was a crack of thunder from the sky and a shaft of lightning shot down towards the brass **conductor**. There was a blue flash, a puff of smoke and Johnny Bullneck's shrill squeak of surprise.

When Timothy dared to look up, rain had stopped play but not a single ball had been bowled. He could just make out the hazy figures of
30　Johnny's gang as they ran screaming across the playing-fields towards the school. At the end of the net lay the frizzy-haired figure of Johnny Bullneck smouldering gently, like a day-old bonfire. In his hands was a blackened trumpet. Around his eyes were two crimson rings where Timothy's glasses had burnt into his flesh.

35　And that's how Johnny Bullneck got fried. The lightning had shot straight down the trumpet and looped the loop round Timothy's metal-framed glasses. I remember the headmaster telling us about it at assembly on Monday morning, but I don't remember a single person crying. Well, it's not as if it's a particularly painful way to go, was it? I
40　mean, it *was* all over in a flash.

More's the pity.

Adapted from *Fat Boy with a Trumpet* by *Jamie Rix*

conductor: *something metal that takes the electricity from the lightning to the ground*

I don't like cricket!

❓ What's it all about?

1 Decide whether each opinion below is right or wrong. Find a quotation to prove your view is correct about each one.

   a In the beginning even the weather seems to be against Timothy.

     Opinion a is right because:
       'The rain pricked Timothy's face like pins.'

   b Johnny doesn't really want Timothy to get hurt.

   c The reader feels sorry for Timothy because he's so helpless.

   d Timothy knew what would happen if Johnny played his trumpet.

   e The way Johnny died serves him right.

Looking at the detail

2 Look at the weather descriptions in lines 3–4, 12–13 and 25–27.

   a Find words in each description to show the weather can hurt people.

   b Who seems most likely to get hurt in the first description?

   c How does this help to make Johnny's death a surprise?

3 Read lines 1–25. Notice how different Johnny and Timothy are.

   a Which of the words below would you use to describe each of them? Use quotations to show why your ideas are right.

> bossy   helpless   confident   afraid
> alone   cunning   cruel   mocking

   b Tension rises as Johnny and Timothy talk in lines 1–22. Copy out and complete the chart below to show how this happens.

What Johnny says	What Timothy says	What the reader realises
	Where's my trumpet?	Timothy has lost something valuable
Safe as houses		Johnny is not to be trusted

4 We do not find out what happened to Johnny straight away.

    a Read lines 23–40. Match up the sentence halves below to explain what happened to Johnny. Then write out the sentences in the right order.

> **D**   going to get hurt and that Johnny is burnt.
>
> **1**   We are told what the headmaster
>
> **2**   Timothy realises he is not
>
> **E**   blowing the trumpet during the storm and squeaking with surprise.
>
> **F**   said had happened to Johnny in assembly.
>
> **3**   We are shown Johnny

    b How does this order build up the surprise of what happened?

? The big question

5 **How does the writer build up to the surprise ending?**

Use your answers to the questions above to help you. In your answer you should comment on:

- the way the weather is used
- the way Johnny and Timothy are described
- the way tension builds as Johnny and Timothy talk
- the way the reader finds out exactly how Johnny died.

Remember

- A writer **shows** rather than tells readers what is happening.
- Tension builds in a story as readers discover little by little what is happening through the **clues** the writer gives them.

Look back at pages 42–47 to find out more about using clues to find out what a text means.

B13 Can't be trusted?

Read the following play extract. Gemma Brogan and her boyfriend Tar have just camped out for the night in a friend's garage. They are both fourteen years old. The scene opens at dawn.

You are going to answer the question:

How does the writer build up a picture of the relationships between Tar, Gemma and their families in this extract?

Liar!

Scene One

Tar	(*to audience*) My name is David. But Gemma calls me Tar, because I always say to her 'Stop smoking or you'll get tar in your lungs.' I'm off. I'm leaving Minely-on-Sea and I'm off to Bristol. My dad beat me up yesterday. It wasn't the first time. Why did he do that? Because I cleaned the house. And my mum? She's too pissed to do it. He was going on at her for using me like a **skivvy**, and she was screaming at him for getting between her and her son. I couldn't win either way. So I'm off. I'm off to Bristol.

Exit Tar with bag.

Gemma	(*to audience*) Last night in the garage, we never did anything. I mean, I wanted to sleep with him. It would have been a nice way to say goodbye, and poor Tar could have done with that. That's to say, if I'd done it before, it would have been a nice way to say goodbye. I only didn't do it for my parents. I wanted to be able to say, look, this was my boyfriend. He was in some really nasty trouble, he'd been beaten up by his dad **for the nth time**, he was running away and I spent the night with him because he needed some company. And I think he might be in love with me. It was just … being close. Now is that human or what? The only thing I regret is that I put my dad before Tar. I won't make that mistake twice.

Scene Two

Gemma, Mr Brogan (Gemma's dad), Mrs Brogan (Gemma's mum).

Mrs Brogan	Your father's right, Gemma, there have to be rules. Surely you can see that?

Gemma	Look … Tar was upset. He just needed someone to stay with him. But there was no sex. Honest. All right?

30 *Pause.*

Mr Brogan	Liar.

Gemma exits to her bedroom, slamming doors.

Gemma	Just … drop down dead! (*To audience*) I locked myself in my room and tried to take the planet over with music.

35

Loud music plays and Gemma dances.

Mr Brogan enters the room and switches the music off.

Mr Brogan	I'm sorry, Gemma, I shouldn't have said that.
Gemma	I'm sorry too. You're still my number one daddy.

40 *Enter Mrs Brogan.*

Mrs Brogan	Have you two made friends now?
Mr Brogan	Oh, yes. Er, we were just discussing what to do next, weren't we, Gemma?

Mrs Brogan puts her arm in Mr Brogan's arm.

45 **Mrs Brogan**	Now you are going to have to do as we say in future, Gemma.
Gemma	Yes, Mum.
Mrs Brogan	You're not going out in the week; me or your father will inspect your homework every evening. And you are forbidden to see David.
50 **Mr Brogan**	Or those louts that hang out by the seafront.
Mrs Brogan	Your other privileges are withdrawn for the time being too, Gemma.
Gemma	What privileges? Breathing? Using the bathroom?
Mrs Brogan	And Friday and Saturday night you can go out but you have to be back by nine o'clock.
55 **Gemma**	Oh, can't we make it half past nine, please?
Mrs Brogan	If you promise to make it half past nine sharp – okay? And the Saturday job is finished.

Gemma opens her mouth – no sound.

Mrs Brogan	Just till you get back on course.
60 **Gemma**	You just think I can't be trusted, but I did everything I could …

Gemma breaks down and cries. Exit Mr Brogan and Mrs Brogan.

Adapted from *Junk* by Melvin Burgess and John Retallack

skivvy: *a servant, usually one who does all the unpleasant work*
for the nth time: *it has happened so often they have lost count*

1 Imagine you are Tar's mum. Describe honestly what happened on the day that Tar left.

2 Imagine you are Mr Brogan. Describe what happened when Gemma returned from the night out.

3 Read lines 45–59. Mrs Brogan is telling Gemma what is going to happen. Make a list of what Gemma's parents have decided to do.

 Looking at the detail

4 Read lines 1–23.

   a Does Tar care about Gemma? How do you know?

   b How does Gemma feel about Tar? How do you know?

5 Read lines 31–37. Why do you think Gemma plays the loud music?

6 Read lines 38–39. Look at how Gemma responds when Mr Brogan says sorry to her. Why do you think she responds like this?

   a She is genuinely sorry and wants to start again.

   b She is embarrassed by what she has done and feels guilty.

   c She is trying to get round her father.

Explain how you made up your mind.

7 Read lines 40–43. Mr Brogan tells Mrs Brogan that they were discussing 'what to do next'. This is not true. Why does Mr Brogan say it?

   a He forgot.

   b He doesn't want to do it because he knows how Gemma will react.

   c He got distracted by Gemma being pleasant to him.

Which do you think is most likely and why?

8 Read lines 45–61. Which punishment hurts most? How do you know?

9 Look at the stage directions on page 111. Find one that makes clear how Mr and Mrs Brogan will stick together in what they do.

10 Tone of voice is very important in a play. The way people say things can alter the meaning in a big way. Read lines 45–57. Write out the speech that you think is said in a sarcastic tone of voice.

? The big question

11 **How does the writer build up a picture of the relationships between Tar, Gemma and their families in this extract?**

In your answer, you should write about:

- how Tar's parents behave
- how Gemma feels and behaves with Tar
- how Gemma reacts to her father
- how Gemma's father responds to her
- how Gemma's mother deals with her
- how Gemma reacts to her mother.

Key points

1 A long speech by one actor in a play or film is called a **monologue**. It allows a character to explain something directly to the audience. If a character is alone on stage, the monologue is called a **soliloquy**.

Can you spot one monologue and one soliloquy in this extract?

- They are both written in the first person: *'I'm off.'*
- They both tell you what the character feels and thinks:

   '… I wanted to sleep with him.'

2 **Stage directions** are important for actors when they perform a play. Look at them carefully when you study a play. They give you hints about what is happening that you might not pick up from the spoken words. For example, this stage direction tells you that Gemma's parents agree about what they are saying:

   Mrs Brogan puts her arm in Mr Brogan's arm.

B14 Mean means beans!

> Read the following transcript. Diane Clarke thinks her husband Nick Clarke is mean with his money. Nick thinks they should not waste money.
>
> You are going to answer the question:
>
> How does Nick Clarke try to prove to Diane Clarke that it is better to buy economy brands rather than named brands?

For richer, for poorer

Diane Clarke Well I noticed he were being mean, when we were courting really. Flowers
5 started drifting off. Chocolates were drifting off. But I really didn't think much of it, you know. And then since we've been
10 married he's got worse. 'Cos like every time I go to the shops and come home we have a row, because he thinks I've brought something we don't need.

Nick Clarke I can't stand spending money needlessly. You go to a supermarket, there's nothing wrong with their
15 economy brands. Buy 'em.

Diane Clarke Yes, there is. Yeah, there is …

Nick Clarke … There's nothing wrong. They're exactly the same …

20 **Diane Clarke** … you can taste the difference, you can …

Nick Clarke … No you can't …

Diane Clarke … between beans and beans and you can tell
25 the difference.

Nick Clarke How can you?

 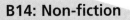

Diane Clarke	Because you can. There's beans and there's beans.
Nick Clarke 30	I've served you up without you, without you knowing …
Diane Clarke	No, get lost …
Nick Clarke	… I've saved tins, empty tins of Heinz Baked Beanz …
35 **Diane Clarke**	No …
Nick Clarke	I've done you beans on toast with Netto's stuff at 7p and I've just showed you empty Heinz Beanz and you've been happy as 40 Larry eating them.
Diane Clarke	No, I'm sorry, I can tell the difference.
Nick Clarke	I'll tell you another one of my favourite scams. You can get Asda Farm Store's Frosted Flakes for seventy-seven pence. And the actual Kelloggs Frosties 45 what the kids insist on having are one pound forty-nine. All I have to do is simply save the box of Frosties and while they're at school, pour the others into the box …
Diane Clarke	That's awful, doing that to your own kids!
Nick Clarke 50	… and then when they see the cereal being poured into dish they think they're getting Frosties, and they've never complained yet and all they're getting are the Frosted Flakes and I'm 72 pence better off in pocket.

Adapted from transcript of _For Richer For Poorer_ by _Siguy Films_

*… three dots is called an **ellipsis.** In written speech it is used to show where someone paused.*

What's it all about?

1 Work in pairs. Prepare a reading of the transcript. Make sure you show that Nick and Diane feel strongly about what they are saying.

2 Diane says Nick is mean. Do you agree? Find two quotations from the text to help you explain why your opinion is right.

Looking at the detail

3 Copy out and complete the chart below. It shows Nick and Diane's different opinions about spending money.

	Nick	Diane
Not buying flowers and chocolates before they were married	I can't stand ...	he were being ...
Buying economy brand baked beans or Heinz baked beans	they're exactly ...	you can taste ...
Giving their children Frosted Flakes rather than Kelloggs Frosties		

4 Read lines 13–40 and 42–52. Think about what Nick says.

   a Diane disagrees with Nick in lines 16 and 48. How does he try to show that he is right each time?

   He tells a ...

   b How does Nick's story prove he is right that it's not worth buying named brands of breakfast cereal?

   c Pick out two phrases which he uses to show that Diane and the children did not notice the difference between brands.

5 Read lines 13–52. Look at how Diane replies to Nick.

   a What does she say to show his story about the beans is not true?

   b How is her argument different about the Frosties?

   She doesn't say ... but she says that what he did was ...

The big question

6   **How does Nick Clarke try to prove to Diane Clarke that it is better to buy economy brands rather than named brands?**

In your answer you should comment on:

- Nick's opinions about spending money
- Diane's opinions about spending money
- How they reply to each other's arguments about buying branded goods
- The proof Nick offers to show he is right.

Key points

A **transcript** shows the words someone actually said. They have not been tidied up to make it easier to read. The chart below shows some of the differences you will find between spoken and written English.

Spoken English	Example	Written English	Example
Incomplete sentences	Yeah there is …	Complete sentences	There is a difference between economy brand and named brand goods.
Informal English	happy as Larry	Formal English	perfectly content
Pauses	… No you can't …	No pauses	No you can't.
Abbreviations	Buy 'em.	No abbreviations	Buy them.

B15 Child with a Cause

Read the poem opposite. It describes something that happened to the poet when she was young.

You are going to answer the question:

How does Moira Andrew show the tensions in the relationships between the characters in this poem?

 ## What's it all about?

1 Read lines 11–14. What mistake does grandmother make?

2 How does grandfather react to the mistake?

3 Read lines 26–28. How does grandmother deal with grandfather's behaviour?

4 The poem is divided into six stanzas (verses) of five lines. Copy and complete this chart. Find one or two phrases to describe each stanza.

Stanza	What it is about
1	Describing Gran
2	
3	
4	
5	
6	

 Remember

A verse in a poem is called a **stanza**.

Child with a Cause

My grandmother was **chicken-plump**
She wore long earrings, smelled of
Pear's soap and lavender water.
She kept cream in a jug under
5   a blue-beaded net.

Grandfather kept us both
on a short rein, our place
at the kitchen sink. When Gran's mind
slipped slightly out of gear
10 I was her memory.

Nearly always, that is. She peeled
potatoes once, put them ready
for Grandfather's tea and forgot
to light the gas. He was furious.
15 I saw Gran's tears.

Upstairs, in the narrow hall
I waited, **scuffing** the turkey-red rug.
He took his time. The flush thundered.
His shape vultured against
20 the door. I was raw

as **carrion**. 'It's not fair.
You made Gran cry.' He lunged at me.
'How dare you, child? How dare you
speak to me like that?' Picked clean
25 by anger I ran.

'Don't mind him,' my grandmother said.
'He likes his tea on time.' The matter
was closed. Grandfather tore into
his beef stew and mashed potatoes.
30 I pushed my plate away.

by Moira Andrew

chicken-plump: *chubby / rounded in a way that reminds you of a chicken*
scuffing: *scraping*
carrion: *dead animal flesh*

5 Read lines 16–17. Why does the child wait upstairs? Put these answers in order. Write down the one you think is best first.

a She is scared so she retreats there.

b She goes there to get out of the way.

c She wants to speak to her grandfather alone.

6 The child faces her grandfather and says:

> 'It's not fair.
> You made Gran cry.'

Choose the words and phrases from the box that you think describe how she feels.

angry   irritated   sensing injustice   worried about what happened concerned for fairness   frustrated   wanting to defend Gran

7 Describe grandfather's reaction to his granddaughter.

8 Look at the way grandfather and the child approach their food. What do you think this tells you about how they are feeling?

9 Good poetry has been described as 'the best words in the best order'. Look at the effect of some of the imagery (word pictures) that Moira Andrew has used. Copy and complete this chart.

Image	Effect
Grandfather kept us both on a short rein (lines 6–7)	The girl and her gran sound like horses that he controls. It suggests they don't have much freedom.
His shape vultured against the door (lines 19–20)	Grandfather looks like a large bird of prey ready to …
I was raw as carrion (lines 20–21)	The writer is seen as being like … She feels …
Picked clean by anger I ran. (lines 24–25)	Grandfather's angry words seem to have eaten into her just as a bird of prey attacks and leaves …

The big question

10 How does Moira Andrew show the tensions in the relationships between the characters in this poem? Write about:

- the grandmother and the girl
- the grandfather and the girl
- the grandmother and grandfather.

Refer to words and phrases in the poem that help to build up a picture of these relationships.

Remember

You need to write down your own comments and thoughts about the poem. You should also use words and phrases from the poem to help you explain how the people feel and behave.

When you copy words from a poem

- copy carefully
- put the words in quotation marks: '...'
- set out lines from a poem so that they look exactly the same as they do in the poem.

Look back at page 56 if you need more help.

B16 Reported!

Read the following police report. It is about an incident that happened in a school, when a boy was seriously injured.

You are going to answer the questions:

- How well does the report tell you what happened? (What are the most important features of a report?)

- Who do you think is to blame for Daniel Hill's injuries?

Nottinghamshire Police Force
Incident Report

Details of main person/s involved

Daniel Hill. Male. Aged 14 (12 January 1986). 22 Ward Street, Ashcroft, Nottinghamshire NG11 2WS

Date and time of incident

5   23 February 2000 – 11.25 a.m.

Place of incident

The Valley School, Park Road, Lower Ashcroft, Nottinghamshire NG11 1ES. Room 128, first floor.

First I received a radio message at 11.41 a.m. to go to an
10   incident at the Valley School in Lower Ashcroft. I arrived at 11.52 a.m. just as an ambulance was leaving the school. It was taking a student, Daniel Hill, to Queen Mary's Hospital. His condition was described as 'serious'. I began my enquiries at 12.05 p.m. by interviewing all those who
15   witnessed the incident.

I next discovered that Daniel Hill had been in an English lesson taught by Mr Andrew Harris. The lesson was taking place in Room 128 on the first floor of the building. At 11.20 a.m. Mr Harris got a message telling him that
20   there was a telephone call for him in the departmental office. The message was from the Headteacher. Mr Harris said that as everyone was working quietly he left the room to go next door to answer the telephone.

I then found out that while Mr Harris was out of the
25 room a student, Anthony Budd, reached into a bag in front
of him and took a pencil case belonging to Katie Hayes,
another member of the class. Budd threw the pencil case
across the room to Hill who went to the window and sat on
the window ledge. He then opened the smaller, upper part of
30 the window and waved the pencil case outside. The two boys,
encouraged by others including Paul Hodges and Adam
Spencer, began to laugh at Katie Hayes. As a result Hill
threatened to drop the pencil case out of the window. This
name-calling had started earlier because Hayes had refused
35 to 'go out' with Budd.

After that Hayes walked towards Hill and asked for the
pencil case back but Hill refused and waved the pencil case
in front of Hayes, who made a grab for it. In the short
struggle that followed, Hayes pushed Hill who then lost his
40 balance and fell backwards towards the window frame from
his sitting position on the ledge. The window frame was in
poor condition and Hill went through it. He landed on a
concrete path about 5 metres below but his fall was partly
broken by a hedge. This was at 11.27 a.m.

45 Later, at 1.40 p.m., I contacted Queen Mary's Hospital.
They told me that Daniel Hill had the following injuries:
broken collar bone, dislocated shoulder, dislocated hip,
broken wrist, three broken fingers, cuts to back of neck,
cheek and shoulder needing 46 stitches, heavy bruising.

50 Finally at 1.50 p.m. I spoke to the Headteacher, Mr
Henry Matthews. He told me that the school had asked the
County Council for new window frames on 12/09/97, 14/05/98
and 21/12/99. Each time they were turned down because the
Council said it did not have enough money for the repairs.
55 The classroom was not closed down because the space was
needed for lessons.

I left the scene at 2.10 p.m.

Signed

Constable D. Peters (34025)

Date
60 27 February 2000

What's it all about?

1 Write down these sentences in the order that they happened.

a Daniel Hill fell out of the window.   **b** Constable Peters arrived.

c Mr Harris left the room.   **d** The pencil case was taken.

e Katie Hayes tried to get her pencil case back.   **f** The ambulance arrived.

Looking at the detail 1

> In a report it is important to get facts in the right order. Words like *first*, *later*, *finally*, *after this* and *next* help to do this. They are called **connect**ives because they **connect** things together and put them in order.

2 Look at your answer to question **1**. Use these connectives to turn the sentences from question **1** into a single piece of writing.

> following this   firstly   and   finally   then   which meant   later

> Reports contain **formal** words. These are the sorts of words that a newsreader uses. You could say that they are 'posh' words. They are used because it is important that reports are not misunderstood.

3 Find a formal word in the report which means the same as:

a an event that's happened (lines 9–15)   **b** asking questions (lines 13–15)

c saw what happened (lines 13–15)   **d** got in touch with (45–49)

e place it all happened (51–57)

The big question 1

4 **How well does the report tell you what happened?** (What are the most important features of a report?)

In your answer you should write about

- **Connectives.** It is important to get things in the right order because … This report …

- **Formal words.** Formal words should be used so that … This report …

Looking at the detail 2

5 The teachers meet in the staff room to read the report. They all have different opinions about who is to blame.

a Read what each teacher says. Then find quotations from the report to support their opinion. The line references show you where to look.

> Well, I think it's Katie's fault because …
> (lines 36–41)

> Daniel Hill has only got himself and his mates to blame. If they hadn't …
> (lines 24–26, 27–30, 30–35)

> Surely Mr Harris should get the blame. I think that …
> (lines 18–23)

> If you think about it, the school and the Council are guilty because …
> (lines 50–54, 55–56)

b Who do you think is most to blame?

The big question 2

6 **Who do you think is to blame for Daniel Hill's injuries?**

In your answer you should:

* include all the facts
* talk about the different opinions of the teachers
* say which opinions you agree with and which you do not agree with. Explain why.

Remember

For help with facts and opinions, look back at pages 36–41.

B17 You'll pay for this ...

Read the following extract about Andi.

You are going to answer the questions:

- **What do you learn from this passage about Andi and her family?**
- **What do you learn about the police in the village where Andi lives?**

Andi's fight

Billi Rosen was born in Greece and later moved to Sweden and then to England. Her first book was about a girl called Andi (short for Antigone). Andi grew up during the Greek Civil War in the 1940s. The war lasted three years and was between the ruling party and the Communist party.

One day at school, Andi starts a fight with Aristo, a policeman's son. He has been bullying other children and stealing their food. At first Aristo is shocked, then he attacks.

Getting hold of my pigtails, he jerked my head back so hard that I was sure it would come clear off my neck. Keeping a tight grip on my hair, he was slowly forcing me to the ground and would have put the boot in had I not sunk my teeth into his plump leg. With a roar of pain he let
5 go of my pigtails and clasped his leg instead. My teeth marks could clearly be seen, and a steady trickle of blood travelled down his leg and on to his neat white socks. 'You'll pay for this, you **red bitch**,' he screamed.

When I got home, I told Grandmother what had happened and asked
10 her why Aristo had called me a 'red bitch'.

'That boy should have his mouth washed out with soap,' snapped Aunt Hercules. Then she turned to me. 'You should be ashamed of yourself, Antigone,' she said. 'Why couldn't you have let things be? Why must you always fight everyone?'

red bitch: *a term of abuse. Red is the Communist party colour – for Aristo, red means the enemy*

15   'But he took their bread,' I protested.

'And who are you to stand up for them? Would anyone have done that for you?'

I looked at Grandmother. 'I was right to fight Aristo, wasn't I?' I asked her.

20   She nodded. 'Yes, my girl. You did right to fight him. He is bad, that one.'

This irritated Aunt Hercules. 'That's right,' she mocked, 'that's right. You just go ahead and encourage her. She'll get us all into trouble one of these days, see if she won't.'

Grandmother waved her to be quiet, then she put her arm around
25 me and pulled me down on to her lap. 'Andi,' she said, 'your aunt is right. Aristo and his people are not like us. A policeman never forgets a wrong. So I'm asking you to be very careful from now on and remember that you haven't made just one enemy but three. By beating Aristo you didn't **humiliate** just him, but his mother and father too. Sooner or
30 later they'll find a way to get even with you … and with us.'

Andi's War by Billi Rosen

humiliate: make someone look small or stupid

What's it all about?

1 Read lines 1–8. What happens in the fight?

2 Which two words from the box best describe the fight? Say why you chose them.

| fair | violent | nasty | surprising | amusing | ordinary |

3 Which two people are there when Andi gets home from school?

Looking at the detail

4 Look at what Aristo says (line 7). What does it tell you about him?

5 Look at what Aunt Hercules says (lines 11–14, 16–17, 21–23). What does it tell you about her?

6 Look at what Grandmother says about Aristo's family (lines 25–30). Write down what she says in your own words.

7 Andi tells Grandmother what has happened at school. Aunt Hercules says what she thinks before Grandmother can say anything. What can you tell from that? Choose the statement that you think is right. Give your reasons.

   a Aunt Hercules is normally quiet.

   b Aunt Hercules likes to give her opinion.

   c Aunt Hercules likes trouble.

8 Who is in charge: Grandmother or Aunt Hercules?

9 How does Grandmother support Andi?

10 Copy and complete this chart. Fill in the name or names that fit each statement.

Statement	Character(s)
Is shocked by bad language	Aunt Hercules
Is a good fighter	
Has a sharp tongue	
Does not understand everything	
Has a sense of justice	
Tries to be comforting	

The big question

11 a **What do you learn from this passage about Andi and her family?**

You should write about:

- Andi's sense of justice
- the way that Andi is willing to fight
- how Aunt Hercules treats Andi
- how Andi's grandmother treats her
- the differences between Aunt Hercules and Andi's grandmother.

b **What do you learn about the police in the village where Andi lives?**

You should write about:

- how Aristo behaves
- what Grandmother says about the police.

Key points

First person narratives

- **Advantage:** You get the story from the angle of the main character. You can see it from their point of view or *viewpoint*. You can get inside their head and feel what they are feeling.

- **Disadvantage:** You only know what is happening inside that one person's head. Your view of other people depends on what that person sees. You don't get the bigger picture.

Building a sense of character

When you read a story, you are not always told what is going on in someone's head. You can build up a picture of the person from three things:

- what they say
- what they do
- what others say about them.

B18 Bus to New York

> Read the passage below carefully. Travel writer Bill Bryson has been staying with his brother in Bloomsburg, which is wealthy, tidy and old-fashioned. He calls it 'pretty well an ideal town'. The journey to New York the next morning is very different.
>
> You are going to answer the question:
>
> How does Bill Bryson get across the idea that the decision to travel by bus is an unpleasant mistake?

On the bus

It was ten minutes to seven in the morning and it was cold. Standing outside the Bloomsburg bus station, I could see my breath. The few cars out this early trailed clouds of **vapour**. I was hung-over and in a few minutes I was going to climb on to a bus for a five-hour ride into
5 New York. I would sooner have eaten cat food.

My brother had suggested that I take the bus because it would save having to find a place to park in Manhattan. I could leave the car with him and come back for it in a day or two. At two in the morning, after many beers, this had seemed a good plan. But now, standing in the
10 early morning chill, I realised I was making a serious mistake. You only go on a long-distance bus in the United States because either you cannot afford to fly or – and this is really licking the bottom of the barrel in America – you cannot afford a car. Being unable to afford a car in America is the last step before living out of a plastic sack.

15 So when the bus pulled up before me, heaving a **pneumatic sigh**, and its door flapped open, I boarded it with some **misgivings**. The driver himself didn't appear any too stable. He had the sort of hair that made him look as if he'd been playing with live wires. There were about half a dozen other passengers, though only two of them looked seriously

---

vapour: gas
pneumatic sigh: hissing noise that coach doors make as they open
misgivings: doubts, fears

20 insane and just one was talking to himself. I took a seat near the back
and settled down to get some sleep. I had drunk far too many beers
with my brother the night before, and the hot spices from my sandwich
were now expanding **ominously** inside my **abdomen** and drifting
around like the stuff they put in **lava lamps**. Soon, from one end or the
25 other, it would begin to **seep out**.

I felt a hand on my shoulder from behind. Through the gap in the
seat I could see it was an Indian man – by that I mean a man from
India, not an American Indian. 'Can I smoke on this bus?' he asked me.

'I don't know,' I said. 'I don't smoke any more, so I don't pay much
30 attention to these things.'

'But do you *think* I can smoke on this bus?'

'I really don't know.'

He was quiet again for a few minutes, then his hand was on my
shoulder again, not tapping it but resting there. 'I can't find an ashtray,'
35 he said.

'No fooling,' I responded wittily, without opening my eyes.

'Do you think that means we're not allowed to smoke?'

'I don't know. I don't care.'

'But do you *think* it means we're not allowed to smoke?'

40 'If you don't take your hand off my shoulder I am going **to dribble
vomit** on it,' I said.

He removed his hand quickly and was silent for perhaps a minute.
Then he said, 'Would you help me look for an ashtray?'

It was seven in the morning and I was deeply unwell. 'WILL YOU
45 PLEASE JUST LEAVE ME ALONE!' I snapped at him, just **a trifle**
wildly. It was going to be a long day.

Adapted from *The Lost Continent* by Bill Bryson

> *ominously:* in a threatening way
> *abdomen:* the lower part of the body
> *lava lamps:* lamps where blobs wobble up and down to create patterns
> *seep out:* ooze out, leak
> *dribble vomit:* to be sick
> *a trifle:* a little

? What's it all about?

1 Read the opening paragraph. What is the weather like?

2 Read lines 6–9. Write out the three statements below that are true.

• There are no parks in Manhattan

• The decision to go by bus was made at two in the morning.

• It was Bill's idea to go by bus and his brother agreed.

• It was his brother's idea to go by bus and Bill agreed.

• The plan to go by bus was dreamed up after several beers.

3 Describe the bus driver in your own words.

4 Imagine you are the man who wants to smoke. Explain what sort of reaction you got from your fellow passenger.

Looking at the detail

5 Read lines 21–25. Bill Bryson could simply have said he felt ill. How does his description tell us more about how he felt?

6 Copy the chart below. Put each quotation with the appropriate comment. The first one is shown for you.

Comment	Quotation
The distaste with which Bill views his five-hour journey is emphasised by a reference to eating. He declares:	a serious mistake.
The sense that bus travel is a bizarre choice is heightened by the description of the driver's hair as making him look	the last step before living out of a plastic sack.
The early morning cold soon convinces Bill that he has made a wrong choice. He describes it as	heaving a pneumatic sigh, and its door flapped open.
Bill exaggerates the horrors of bus travel by describing it as	I would sooner have eaten cat food.
The feeling that the bus is some sort of elderly and not very pleasant creature is created by the way it pulls up	as if he'd been playing with live wires.

7 Find the six responses Bill Bryson uses to try to silence the passenger behind him. Write them out. Describe how you think he said each sentence.

8 **How does Bill Bryson get across the idea that the decision to travel by bus is an unpleasant mistake?**

In your answer you should write about:

- the weather as he waits for the bus
- how the choice of travel was made
- the bus driver
- Bill Bryson's state of health
- phrases that communicate his dislike of this kind of travel
- his growing anger with the passenger behind him.

Key points

Travel writers usually include four things:

- descriptions of places
- descriptions of people
- accounts of the actual journeys
- stories about what happens along the way.

Much travel writing works by contrasts. These are often between places or between people. In this passage the author's feelings about the bus station in the early morning are in contrast to his view of Bloomsburg.

You can also see how people thrown together behave. Bill Bryson wants to be ill in silence and not communicate with anyone. The man behind him on the bus clearly wants to talk.

B19 Man or beast?

Read the following passage. Dr Jekyll has warned his friend, Dr Lanyon, to expect a visitor. He has asked Dr Lanyon to give the visitor some powders. Soon, the strange visitor arrives …

You are going to answer the question:

How does the writer build up the idea that Dr Lanyon's visitor is strange and unusual?

The visitor

The knocker sounded very gently on the door. I went and found a small man crouching against the wall.

'Are you come from Dr Jekyll?' I asked.

5 He told me 'Yes.' He entered and I followed him into the bright light of the room. Here, I had a chance of clearly seeing him. I had never set eyes on him before, that was certain. He was small, as I have said; I was struck with the shocking expression of his face. His clothes were enormously too large for him in every measurement – the trousers hanging on his legs and rolled up to keep them from the ground. There
10 was something abnormal about the creature facing me, something revolting.

'Have you got it?' he cried. 'Have you got it?'

'There it is, sir,' said I, pointing to where it lay on the floor behind a table. He sprang to it, and then paused, and laid his hand upon his
15 heart; I could hear his teeth grate and his face was so ghastly to see that I grew alarmed.

'Have you a glass?' he asked. I rose from my place and gave him what he asked.

He thanked me, measured out a few drops of the red liquid and
20 added one of the powders. The mixture, which was at first reddish, began to brighten in colour, effervesce noisily and throw off small fumes of vapour. Suddenly it changed to a dark purple, which faded again more slowly to a watery green.

He put the glass to his lips, and drank at one gulp. A cry followed; he
25 reeled, staggered, clutched at the table and held on, staring with
infected eyes, gasping with open mouth; and as I looked, there came a
change – he seemed to swell – his face became suddenly black, and the
features seemed to melt and alter – and the next moment I had sprung
to my feet and leaped back against the wall, my arm raised to shield
30 me from that terror.

'O God!' I screamed, and 'O God!' again and again; for there before
my eyes – pale and shaken, and half fainting, and groping before him
with his hands, like a man restored from death – there stood Henry
Jekyll!

Adapted from *The Strange Case of Dr Jekyll and Mr Hyde*
by Robert Louis Stevenson

A small man knocked on the door …

There was something abnorm
about the creature facing m
something revolting.

Are you from Dr Jekyll?

He … measured out a few drops of the red liquid …

He drank at one gulp …

'Have you got it?' he cried.
'There it is, sir,' said I, pointing to where it lay ...

3

6

There came a change ...

I leaped back in terror.

'O God'

What's it all about?

1 Read the graphic version of the passage on the pages 136–137. Each picture has a few words from the passage to go with it. Choose and write out one whole sentence from the story to go with each of the pictures.

Looking at the detail

2 Read the key points on page 139. Read these lines again, then answer the questions.

   a Line 4: *He* told me 'Yes.'   Who is '**he**'?

   b Line 9: *keep **them** from the ground.*   What is '**them**'?

   c Line 22: *Suddenly **it** changed.*   What changed?

   d Line 33: *with **his** hands.*   Whose hands?

3 There may be some words in this passage that you do not know. What do you think the words listed below mean? Read the words slowly and carefully. Use the rest of the sentence and the passage to help you. Look back at pages 58–61 if you need more help.

   a expression (line 7)   **d** effervesce (line 21)   **g** features (line 28)

   b abnormal (line10)   **e** vapour (line 22)   **h** groping (line 32)

   c ghastly (line 15)   **f** reeled (line 25)   **i** restored (line 33)

4 Choose two words from question **3** to describe the strange looks of the visitor. Then choose two words to describe his strange actions.

5 Answer these questions about the visitor's strange looks and actions.

Strange looks

   a How is the visitor's expression described? (line 7)

   b What is unusual about his clothes? (lines 7–9)

   c How is the 'creature' described? (lines 9–11)

Strange actions

   d What is the visitor doing when the door is answered? (line 2)

   e What did Dr Lanyon hear? (line 15)

   f What does the visitor do with the powders? (lines 19–20)

6 Read lines 24–30 carefully. What happens when the mixture is drunk? Write a list of all the things that happen as the change takes place.

7 **How does the writer build up the idea that Dr Lanyon's visitor is strange and unusual?**

In your answer you should write about:

- the way the visitor looks and acts when he first arrives
- what happens to him when he drinks the mixture
- the words that make him seem unusual.

Remember to use quotations from the passage to support what you say.

Key points

Pronouns are words that are used instead of nouns (names), for example:

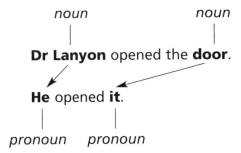

The following words are pronouns:

it, he, she, we, they, I, me, you, him, her, us, them, his, hers, our.

It is sometimes difficult to understand what is happening in a passage. It can help to look at each pronoun to work out exactly what is happening and who is speaking.

C1 Test 1

This unit gives you practice at answering the sorts of questions you might meet in a test. Below are some tips to help you to show what you know and to give your best answer.

TIP 1 First read the instructions carefully. Different tests have different instructions. The number of questions and the marks for each question may change. You may have more or less time to do the test. Make sure you know exactly what you have to do.

---

1 Read the instructions below. Then answer the questions to check you have understood them.

You have 15 minutes to read the test paper and make notes. You may not begin writing your answers until you are told.

Then you have 1 hour and 30 minutes to write your answers.

Answer all the questions in Sections A and B.

Choose one question from Section C.

You should spend **about 20 minutes on question 1 (worth 9 marks)**
10 minutes on question 2 (worth 6 marks)
20 minutes on question 3 (worth 15 marks)
35 minutes on question 4 (worth 20 marks)
5 minutes checking your work.

---

a How long must you spend reading the test paper and making notes?

b How long do you have to write your answers?

c How many questions must you answer?

d Which question should you spend longest on?

TIP 2 Remember to use PQRS each time you have to read a text and answer questions on it.

Look back at pages 10–15 for more help.

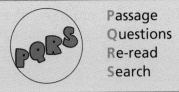

Passage
Questions
Re-read
Search

2   How can you use PQRS to help you read a test paper?

TIP 3 **Break questions down**

- Break each question down into smaller parts. If there are bullet points, use them as a guide to what you should write about in your answer.

- In the exam you could underline the main parts of a question. Look for key words. This will help you remember what your answers must cover.

- Make notes about the information and ideas in the text you will use when you write about each bullet point. (You will learn more on how to do this later.)

- In the exam you can underline the parts of the passage you will use in your answer.

3   A student has copied out a question and underlined key words.
     Say why they have underlined each one.

Refer to words and phrases in the passage to support your ideas.

1   **How does the writer build a picture of Tar's life as a runaway?**

In your answer you should comment on:

- the way Tar describes sleeping on the streets

- the way he describes sleeping in 'Hotel d'Erelict'

- the way he tries to improve his room

- the reasons why he goes to buy a bar of chocolate.

I must remember to:

1   Find at least one short quotation to support my answer for each bullet point.

2   Look for descriptions that build up the picture of Tar's life.

3   Make sure I write something about each bullet point.

Use the skills you have learned and practised in this book as you work through the practice test questions that follow.

4   Below are the questions you are going to answer on the following passage. Use the steps on pages 146–147 to help you tackle these sorts of questions on your own.

Read the passage opposite. Then answer questions 1 and 2.
Spend 20 minutes on question 1 and 10 minutes on question 2.

Refer to words and phrases in the passage to support your ideas.

1   **How does the writer build a picture of Tar's life as a runaway?**

In your answer you should comment on:

- the way Tar describes sleeping on the streets

- the way he describes sleeping in 'Hotel d'Erelict'

- the way he tries to improve his room

- the reasons why he goes to buy a bar of chocolate.   *(11 marks)*

2   **What impression do you get of Joe Scholl's attitude towards homeless people?**

In your answer you should comment on:

- the way Tar describes him

- the way he speaks to Tar.   *(6 marks)*

Tar has run away from home. He wants his girlfriend to come and join him.

The runaway

The first couple of nights I slept out in doorways. The very first night I tried to go to sleep in my bag in the doorway of a small supermarket but it was too cold. I ended up wandering around all night. Towards morning I saw people crowded
5 together in a subway, all wrapped up in cardboard boxes, and I thought, That's how you do it! And I wandered about some more till I found some cardboard in stacks outside a shop waiting for the binmen. I wrapped myself up in that, and that was better. But you still keep waking up all night. You never
10 seem to get a decent night's sleep on the street.

   I slept like that for a couple of nights, but I didn't like it on the street. For one thing you're in public. People can see you all the time, even when you're asleep. Sometimes at night you wake up and the police are shining a torch into your face. I
15 hated that – the thought of people examining you while you're asleep, all those strangers. I began to feel like something in a zoo. So when I found this row of **derry** houses, I thought, Right. This is gonna be home.

   I found a little room with a door still on it. The first night I
20 kept getting woken up by people banging in. It was pitch black so they couldn't see me till I called out. It happened about five times that night. I was really scared the first few times, but after a bit I realised it was just people looking for a place to sleep. I shouted out, 'It's taken,' and they left.

25 The next day I made a little sign: 'Do Not Disturb.' And I wrote, 'Property of Hotel d'Erelict' in little letters underneath.

   Everyone had to find their way with matches or a torch, so they all saw my sign and I never got bothered after that. Just a couple of times some drunks came charging in without
30 seeing my notice. Sometimes they thought it was so funny they'd wake me up.

---

derry: *short for derelict, which means that no one looks after it*

'Will you leave your boots outside for cleaning?' someone yelled. And, 'Will Sir require his breakfast in bed?' That sort of thing. That was okay.

35 It was out of the open but it was a right mess in there. People had dumped binbags full of rubbish, waste paper, old clothes, even rubble. I slept on top of it for a few nights. I suppose I was feeling depressed. I was thinking a lot about my mum.

40 Then I thought. Get on with it.

First of all I scooped all the rubbish into binbags and carried it out round the back. I pinched the binbags from someone's dustbin. I found a broken broom in a skip and gave the room a good brush down. It was still a tip, but at least it 45 was a brushed tip.

Since then I'd been collecting bits and pieces – a few wooden crates, a bit of carpet someone chucked out. I couldn't make it too nice because someone would have nicked stuff or wrecked it. But I'd tried to make it mine.

50 I was on my way back to the squat now. On the way I had to go past Joe Scholl's tobacconist. I thought I'd go in and have a Twix. Have a treat. I completely forgot about begging. You do. You just forget, you buy a bar of chocolate and then you think, Oh no …

55 Joe Scholl's a nice man. He'd given me a few quid a couple of times in the past few days. I think he gave quite a bit of money to people on the street.

'You look full of the joys today, David,' he said.

'Yeah. My girlfriend's coming to stay,' I told him. I think I 60 only went in there so I could tell someone the news.

I took a Twix bar and dug in my pocket for the money. He didn't laugh, but then he never did. He always kept his face completely straight, except his eyebrows were permanently up in the air. You hardly ever saw him move his face, even when 65 he was cracking you up with laughter. Deadpan.

'That's good news then.' He didn't take my money. He just looked at me. 'Leaving her folks like you did, is she?' he wanted to know.

I looked at him. 'Yeah ...'

70   'How old is she, then, David?'

I didn't dare tell him how old she really was. I said, 'Sixteen.' That's how old I'd told him I was. I started eating the Twix to hide my embarrassment.

'Nice.' He stood there with his hands hanging by his sides
75 watching me. 'Where you putting her up, then? Honeymoon suite in the Hotel Derry?'

'Yeah ...'

Adapted from *Junk* *by Melvin Burgess*

5   Follow these three steps and learn how to tackle any question.

STEP 1

Look at question **1** on page 142 again. What does each bullet point
guide you to think about? Jot down line numbers from the passage for
each one, to use in your answer.

STEP 2

For each point make a chart like the one below to help you work out
your answer. Jot your ideas down in note form to save time.

- the way Tar describes sleeping on the streets

This detail (clue)	shows that	which suggests
Lines 3–4: too cold; wandering all night	Very uncomfortable	Gets no sleep, always tired
Lines 5–6: I thought, That's how you do it	Finds out for himself	Nobody cares, lonely
Line 11: You're in public	People can see you	No privacy
Line 15: Feels like something in a zoo	Like an animal	Not a person

STEP 3

Now write your answer to question **1** on page 142. Use your charts to
help you.

6   Now read question **2** on page 142 again. Then follow the three steps
you have just learned to plan and write your answer.

'I want to see you have understood the text. I don't just want you to copy it out.'

... so remember to follow these three steps when you are writing about a text.

details +	give us a clue +	which suggests
choose information from the text	show what it means	explain how it answers the question
'... but you still keep waking up all night.'	Tar never gets a whole night's sleep.	Living on the streets is hard because you are always tired.

Look back at pages 42–47 for more help.

7 When you write an answer, bear in mind what an examiner is looking for. Read what three students have written as part of their answers to question **1**. Give the best answer A, the second best B and the worst C. Give reasons for your choices.

1   Tar tells you it's too cold to sleep on the streets. Then the Hotel Derelict is awful as well. He keeps getting drunks walking into his room. He tries to make his room nicer but he doesn't want to do much or someone will wreck it. He goes to buy a bar of chocolate because he is feeling happy.

2   Tar makes life as a runaway sound awful because he has to sleep in some awful places.

3   The text says that it is impossible to 'get a decent night's sleep' on the street. This means Tar would always be tired which would make life awful. It is cold too. Tar has to search for cardboard to keep warm. He hasn't got enough shelter. This makes life as a runaway really hard.

Even when Tar finds a room in a derelict house he is not safe. Sometimes drunks come 'charging in' which must be frightening. He can only clear his room up a bit because: 'someone would have nicked stuff or wrecked it.'

Tar is lonely living on the streets too. That's why he buys the bar of chocolate. So he can have a chat with Mr Scholl.

Now use the skills you have learned and practised in this book as you work through the practice test questions on a non-fiction exercise.

Read the leaflet on the following pages. Then answer question 1. You have 30 minutes to answer this question.

It is a leaflet explaining the work The Children's Society does with runaway children who are living on the streets.

Refer to words and phrases in the passage to support your ideas.

1 **How does the leaflet persuade people to give money to support the work of The Children's Society?**

In your answer you should comment on:

- the information the leaflet gives about what £5 can do
- the way the work of The Children's Society is described
- the way words and layout are used to make you feel sorry for runaway children
- whether the leaflet will persuade people to give money to The Children's Society.

TIP 1 Since this is a non-fiction leaflet, as you read it look for:

HIP See pages 16–23.

and

PA and MA + See pages 24–29.

TIP 2 Follow steps 1, 2 and 3 on page 146 to help you plan and write your answer.

STEP 1
Re-read the question. What does each bullet point guide you to think about? Jot down line numbers to use in your answer.

STEP 2
For each bullet point make a chart under the headings below to help you work out your answer.

This detail (clue)	shows that	which suggests

STEP 3
Now write your answer to question **1**. Use your charts to help you.

£5 could buy this street survival kit...

shampoo
soap
flannel
toothpaste
toothbrush
underwear
socks
chocolate bar   0.30
coin for telephone   0.10
gloves   0.80
                       5.00

£5 doesn't buy much these days. It's less than the price of a paperback book or a cinema ticket. But in the hands of The Children's Society it could help save the life of a runaway child.

5 Because £5 could pay for the cost of providing a Street Survival Kit. The kit holds essentials like toothpaste, clean underwear and some high-energy foods such as chocolate or nuts. It can help make life on the streets bearable. More

10 importantly, it can be used by our street workers to make contact with children in real need.

When we hand out these kits, it gives us an opportunity to start a conversation. With careful handling that conversation can turn into a

15 relationship. And once that has happened, our workers can begin the real job of getting those children off the streets and into safe accommodation. It's only one further step to begin rebuilding these children's lives.

20 The Children's Society has been working with disadvantaged children since 1881. In our 119-year history we have learnt a great deal about what children need to get the best start in life and we regularly put this

25 understanding into practice. We give runaway children safe **refuges**, we ensure that children are educated rather than **excluded** from school, and we also support programmes that offer children a safe place

30 to live and grow up in.

By supporting the work of The Children's Society you will ensure **vulnerable** children get the help they need.

> ‘ *The Children's Society listened to me and they cared. That made a difference because, before that, I didn't really think anyone cared if I lived or died.* ’
>
> Rachel, 16 years old.

Buy a street survival kit for a runaway child.

Send a gift of £5 today.

---

refuge: *a safe place to live*   ***excluded:*** *kept out*   ***vulnerable:*** *easily hurt*

Test 2

You have 10 minutes to read the test paper and to make notes. You must not start to write your answers until you are told.

Then you have 55 minutes to write your answers.

You should answer **all** the questions.

You should spend **about 5 minutes on question 1**
15 minutes on question 2
10 minutes on question 3
20 minutes on question 4
5 minutes checking your work.

Ask your teacher if you are not sure what to do.

Section A

Read the following passage.

Then answer questions 1, 2 and 3 on page 155.

fatal: deadly

Jane Goldman's book *Sussed and Streetwise* gives advice for young people about staying safe. The book includes what teenagers say as well as what Jane thinks. This extract looks at getting around safely.

DON'T RISK IT: travel at night

There are lots of things to think about when you're going out – what to wear, how to get there, what you're going to do. It's not really surprising if you don't give much thought to how you're going to get home. This can be a **fatal** mistake to make. We all
5   know how dangerous it can be to be stranded in the dark, especially if you're not sure where you are or how to get back, and yet so many people find themselves in that situation so often.

Ideally, planning how you're going to get home should be something you do automatically, every time you go out. With all
10   that other stuff on your mind, it can be a hard habit to get into, but it's very important that you do. At best, being stranded is annoying, confusing and a bit scary. At worst, it could mean being followed, threatened or attacked. Either way, it's a horrible way to end a great evening out – and if you actually get attacked, that's
15   going to be putting it mildly!

Once you're in the habit of planning your return journeys, you've taken a big step on the road to safety. But how you choose to travel is obviously very important too.

You need to be especially careful getting around alone at
20   night. I'm sure we all agree that this is a stupid, terrible state of affairs, and that everybody should have the right to walk around freely at any time of the day or night without the fear of anything bad happening to them, but that's just the way things are, unfortunately. 'Standing up for your rights' by walking home on
25   your own or waiting alone at a **deserted** bus stop in the middle of the night isn't going to change a thing.

fatal: *deadly*
deserted: *empty, without anyone else around*

'My mum told me that when she was young, boys always came and collected you before a date and then took you home afterwards. Even if they didn't have a car, they would come to your
30 house anyway, just so you didn't have to travel on your own. She couldn't believe that boys don't normally do that any more, especially now that it's more dangerous for a girl to get around on her own in the dark. But then, it can be dangerous for boys, too.'

Anna, 14

35 'He lived in my block of flats, so we'd always taken the bus home together after we'd been out. Then one night – it was our fourth date, I think – he said he was staying at his dad's for the weekend, which meant that he had to take a different bus. Our block is miles away from the bus stop and you have to walk past
40 all these creepy alleyways, so it's really dangerous if you're on your own. I was okay, thank God, but after that, I always asked him before we went out whether he was coming back to his mum's or not, so that I could get a lift home instead if he wasn't.'

Cass, 15

45 Planning **the outward leg of your journey** shouldn't be too much hassle – arrange to meet at a familiar, easy-to-reach spot.

Planning how you're going to get home can be more difficult. Whereas it used to be traditional for boys to walk girls home after a date, it's not really fair to expect that now – after all, the
50 streets can be dangerous for boys alone too.

The safest way to travel around in the evening alone is by car, so if your parents drive and are prepared to pick you up, it makes a lot of sense to take them up on their offer. However, even this can be tricky to arrange if you don't know exactly where you're
55 going on the date, or what time exactly you'll finish. And of course, there's all that embarrassment stuff, but in this case it makes a lot of sense to be very mature about it and put your safety first.

Adapted from *Sussed and Streetwise* by Jane Goldman

the outward leg of your journey: *the first part: getting to the event*

Section A questions

1. Read lines 27–33. What do you learn about how going out on a date has changed over the years? *(3 marks)*

2. Look at the whole passage. What do you learn about staying safe on dates? *(9 marks)*

3. Look at the whole passage. Jane Goldman uses two teenage writers as well as herself. What do they contribute to the subject? *(6 marks)*

Section B

Read the passage below.

Then answer question 4 on page 158.

Lydia wants to join Anne's gang. In order to join the gang, Lydia's 'friend' Anne has dared her to take the school's big silver sports cup. She has to keep it for a day and then put it back. Lydia stays behind after school to take a look at the cup. This scene starts during assembly on the next morning.

Taking a risk

'Would Lydia Henson please stay behind?'

It was an order, not a request. The headmaster's words stopped all whispers in the hall. Lydia was suddenly drowning under the weight of the stares of those around her. She felt
5   totally sick. She looked around **dismayed**, then across the hall to where Mr Simmers stood. Why had he asked her to stay behind? What was going on? Lydia tried to catch Anne's eye, but Anne looked straight ahead as she waited for her row to be allowed to leave the hall.

10   Lydia waited for the rest of the school to **amble** out. She kept her head bent, unable to meet the curious glances directed at her. Then she moved slowly down to the front of the hall. Mr Simmers stood on the stage, towering over her like a New York skyscraper next to a beetle.

15   'Do you have something you wish to tell me, Lydia?' he asked.

Lydia's 'No, sir' was stuck somewhere between her tongue and the roof of her mouth. She shook her head slowly.

'Follow me,' commanded Mr Simmers.

The headmaster strode out of the hall, not bothering to look
20   at Lydia. Lydia followed him – she could do nothing else. Why

dismayed: *frightened or alarmed*   **amble:** *walk slowly*

had he picked her out? If only Lydia could have spoken to Anne – just for a minute. She longed to know what was going on, but who could she ask? Certainly not Mr Simmers. He looked as if his head was about to explode. Maybe he knew about her being in the hall late the previous afternoon after school. Maybe Old Baldie the caretaker had told him and Mr Simmers just wanted to talk to her about who else she might have seen around at the same time.

To Lydia's surprise, Mr Simmers didn't lead the way to his office but instead turned right. Lydia wondered where they were going. She didn't have to wait long to find out. The girls' cloakroom. Lydia had to trot to keep up with Mr Simmers' long stride. Once inside, they turned down the second aisle to the left of the cloakroom doors and Lydia saw Mrs Irving and Mr Balding ahead. The cloakroom was almost steaming with warm, damp coats hanging on coat hooks up and down the aisles. At last Mr Simmers came to an abrupt halt.

The headmaster and Mr Balding looked at each other. Mr Balding nodded almost **imperceptibly**.

'Lydia Henson, is this your locker?' Mr Simmers pointed to the locker in front of him but his eyes never left Lydia's face.

Lydia tried to speak but the words got lost in her throat. She swallowed, then tried again.

'Yes, sir.' The words came out as a frightened squeal.

'Open it,' Mr Simmers ordered.

Lydia looked at all three of the grown-ups before looking at her locker. They all looked poised, as if one false move on her part and they would pounce, tearing her to pieces. Lydia's heart **pummelled** her ribs. What was wrong? What was going on?

Wiping her clammy hands on her skirt, she walked forward. She reached out to the combination lock on her locker door before realising that the locker door was shut but not locked.

'It's open,' she said, surprised.

imperceptibly: *so it could not be noticed*
pummelled: *kept thumping away at*

'Mr Balding has been opening all the lockers in here and in the boys' cloakroom on my instructions,' said Mr Simmers. 'I had
55 reason to believe that the sports cup would still be on the school premises.'

Lydia stared from her locker to Mr Simmers' stony face and back again. Her eyes widened to their absolute limits.

'I don't have it. I don't have the cup,' she said, aghast.

60 'Open your locker, Lydia,' Mr Simmers repeated grimly.

Lydia slowly reached out for the door handle. It was cool beneath her fingertips. She swallowed hard. She could hear Mr Balding wheezing in the background. The sound came from far away. She had to strain to hear it. Immediately around her was
65 silence. A sudden sound, like bucketfuls of gravel being thrown onto the flat roof of the girls' cloakroom, made Lydia jump. Outside, the rain, which had been bad enough before, was now tipping down. A smell like damp towels came from all the coats. Lydia's mouth was dry. Her palms were clammy. She grasped the
70 locker handle and pulled it open. A glint of silver dazzled her. It took a few moments for Lydia to focus. And there, in front of her PE kit and her scarf and gloves – was the sports cup.

Adapted from *Thief* by Malorie Blackman

Section B questions

4   **How does the writer build up the tension in Lydia's situation?**

In your answer, you should comment on:

* the effect of Mr Simmers asking her to stay behind
* what happens once Lydia and Mr Simmers have left the assembly hall
* the scene in front of the lockers.

Refer to words and phrases in the passage to support your ideas.   *(11 marks)*

Glossary

alliteration	words in a poem which begin with the same letter or sound and are close together: *the raging river roared.* (See page 50)
appeal	an advertisement's **appeal** is the reason readers will want the product it is offering: *because it will make me look good.* (See page 28)
audience	the group of people a text is written for. (See page 6)
conflict	the struggle between characters or ideas, or the problem which has to be overcome at the beginning of a story: *the main character wants to win an Olympic medal but he is very unfit.* (See page 12)
contrast	the difference pointed out between two things.
couplets	two lines of poetry that come together. When they rhyme they are a **rhyming couplet**. (See page 78)
description	writing that tells you what something is like. (See page 88)
development of problem	the **middle** part of the story where you find out more about the problem. (See page 12)
dialogue	conversation spoken by characters. (See page 88)
fact	something that can be checked or proved to be true: *the Earth is round.* (See page 36)
fiction	writing which has 'made up' events in it, such as a story. It often follows the pattern **conflict–development– resolution**. (See page 11)
first person	The story is written from one person's point of view as if the writer is that person. *I knew there was something going on.* (See page 92)
imagery	pictures created by words to help the reader to imagine what the writer is describing. (See page 52)
metaphor	an image where the writer makes it sound as if a thing *actually is* something else. The words *as* or *like* are not used: *His fur was a matted carpet.* (See page 52)
monologue	a speech given by one character in a play or film. (See page 113)
narrative	the telling of a story.

onomatopoeia	a word whose sound echoes its meaning: *rustling, crackled.*
opinion	someone's point of view. (See page 36)
plot	the events that take place in a story.
purpose	why the writer has written the text. (See page 8)
quotation	words which you have copied out from the text into your work (see pages 56–57 for more on quoting).
repetition	when the same word or phrase is repeated. (See page 94)
the resolution	the **end** of the story where the problem comes to an end (one way or another). (See page 12)
rhyme	words which end in the same sounds: *log, frog.* (See page 48)
rhythm	the beat of the words in a line: *rockin' rollin' divin' slidin'.* (See page 50)
setting	where and when the events take place.
simile	an image where two things are compared using the words *as* or *like: My feet were like lumps of ice.* (See page 52)
stage direction	the words that tell actors how to behave while they say the words. (See page 111)
stanza or verse	a group of lines in a poem. (See page 48)
tension	the feeling that something important is about to happen. (See page 72)
third person	the story is written by someone who sees the events from the outside.
tone	the mood or feeling of a piece of writing: *funny, persuasive, sad.*
viewpoint	the point of view from which the story is told. (See page 127)